CONTROVERSIES

Soft Power and Diplomacy

Other Books in the Current Controversies Series

Current
CONTROVERSIES

Soft Power and Diplomacy

Bridey Heing, Book Editor

GREENHAVEN
PUBLISHING

Published in 2020 by Greenhaven Publishing, LLC
353 3rd Avenue, Suite 255, New York, NY 10010

Copyright © 2020 by Greenhaven Publishing, LLC

First Edition

Articles in Greenhaven Publishing anthologies are often edited for length to meet page
requirements. In addition, original titles of these works are changed to clearly present
the main thesis and to explicitly indicate the author's opinion. Every effort is made to
ensure that Greenhaven Publishing accurately reflects the original intent of the authors.
Every effort has been made to trace the owners of the copyrighted material.

Cover image: Alexandros Michailidis/Shutterstock.com

Library of Congress Cataloging-in-Publication Data

Names: Heing, Bridey, editor.
Title: Soft power and diplomacy / Bridey Heing, book editor.
Description: New York : Greenhaven Publishing, 2020. | Series: Current
  controversies | Audience: Grades: 9 to 12. | Includes bibliographical
  references and index.
Identifiers: LCCN 2018061347| ISBN 9781534505421 (library bound) | ISBN
  9781534505438 (pbk.)
Subjects: LCSH: International relations—Juvenile literature. |
  Diplomacy—Juvenile literature.
Classification: LCC JZ1305 .S664 2020 | DDC 327.2—dc23
LC record available at https://lccn.loc.gov/2018061347

Manufactured in the United States of America

Website: http://greenhavenpublishing.com

Contents

Chapter 1: Does Soft Power Positively Influence International Affairs?

Jan Melissen

Melissen argues that international relations in the twentieth and twenty-first centuries have been shaped more by public diplomacy than by traditional state diplomacy, a change that experts are still learning how to manage.

Yes: Soft Power Benefits International Peace

Francesca Centracchio

Centracchio shows how soft power has allowed Brazil, an emerging power, to gain influence in business, international affairs, and culture, making a case for why soft power is the dominant force for diplomacy in the twenty-first century.

David Ensor

Ensor argues that soft power can shape political action, using the example of US coverage of ISIS war crimes and the ways in which such coverage drove awareness and state policy.

No: Soft Power Exacerbates Power Imbalances Between States

Michael Cecire

Looking at the annexation of Crimea by Russia, Cecire argues that the Ukraine crisis highlights the weaknesses of soft power and the difficulty in leveraging it in the face of hard power.

No: Diplomacy Does Not Allow a State to Exert Influence Meaningfully

Chapter 3: Has Social Media Had a Positive Influence on Diplomacy?

Yes: Social Media Allows for New Forms of Public Diplomacy

Yes: Diplomacy and Military Power Complement One Another

William Inboden

Inboden argues that military strength and diplomatic strategy complement one another, and that both are necessary to establish and build on US interests abroad.

Senator Rand Paul and Isaac Applbaum

The authors argue that in a world where diplomatic alliances change rapidly, hard and soft power are important tools to help ensure US security and interests.

Joseph Nye

Nye asserts that in the present era, military power alone is not enough for the United States to succeed in international conflicts. Instead, it must also use its economic and cultural influence to its advantage. Given the wide range of variables that impact international relations today, economic, military, and soft power all play a role.

No: Diplomacy and Hard Power Are Mutually Exclusive Tools

Phyllis Bennis

Bennis highlights cases in which diplomacy, rather than military action, has successfully averted conflict or helped build working relationships between states.

Nathan Gardels

Gardels argues that China's strength on the international stage is built on soft power but that forays into hard power have undermined that foundation to the detriment of Chinese influence.

Foreword

Controversy is a word that has an undeniably unpleasant connotation. It carries a definite negative charge. Controversy can spoil family gatherings, spread a chill around classroom and campus discussion, inflame public discourse, open raw civic wounds, and lead to the ouster of public officials. We often feel that controversy is almost akin to bad manners, a rude and shocking eruption of that which must not be spoken or thought of in polite, tightly guarded society. To avoid controversy, to quell controversy, is often seen as a public good, a victory for etiquette, perhaps even a moral or ethical imperative.

Yet the studious, deliberate avoidance of controversy is also a whitewashing, a denial, a death threat to democracy. It is a false sterilizing and sanitizing and superficial ordering of the messy, ragged, chaotic, at times ugly processes by which a healthy democracy identifies and confronts challenges, engages in passionate debate about appropriate approaches and solutions, and arrives at something like a consensus and a broadly accepted and supported way forward. Controversy is the megaphone, the speaker's corner, the public square through which the citizenry finds and uses its voice. Controversy is the life's blood of our democracy and absolutely essential to the vibrant health of our society.

Our present age is certainly no stranger to controversy. We are consumed by fierce debates about technology, privacy, political correctness, poverty, violence, crime and policing, guns, immigration, civil and human rights, terrorism, militarism, environmental protection, and gender and racial equality. Loudly competing voices are raised every day, shouting opposing opinions, putting forth competing agendas, and summoning starkly different visions of a utopian or dystopian future. Often these voices attempt to shout the others down; there is precious little listening and considering among the cacophonous din. Yet listening and considering, too, are essential to the health of a democracy. If controversy is democracy's lusty lifeblood, respectful listening and careful thought are its higher faculties, its brain, its conscience.

Current Controversies does not shy away from or attempt to hush the loudly competing voices. It seeks to provide readers with as wide and representative as possible a range of articulate voices on any given controversy of the day, separates each one out to allow it to be heard clearly and fairly, and encourages careful listening to each of these well-crafted, thoughtfully expressed opinions, supplied by some of today's leading academics, thinkers, analysts, politicians, policy makers, economists, activists, change agents, and advocates. Only after listening to a wide range of opinions on an issue, evaluating the strengths and weaknesses of each argument, assessing how well the facts and available evidence mesh with the stated opinions and conclusions, and thoughtfully and critically examining one's own beliefs and conscience can the reader begin to arrive at his or her own conclusions and articulate his or her own stance on the spotlighted controversy.

This process is facilitated and supported in each Current Controversies volume by an introduction and chapter overviews that provide readers with the essential context they need to begin engaging with the spotlighted controversies, with the debates surrounding them, and with their own perhaps shifting or nascent opinions on them. Chapters are organized around several key questions that are answered with diverse opinions representing all points on the political spectrum. In its content, organization, and methodology, readers are encouraged to determine the authors' point of view and purpose, interrogate and analyze the various arguments and their rhetoric and structure, evaluate the arguments' strengths and weaknesses, test their claims against available facts and evidence, judge the validity of the reasoning, and bring into clearer, sharper focus the reader's own beliefs and conclusions and how they may differ from or align with those in the collection or those of classmates.

Research has shown that reading comprehension skills improve dramatically when students are provided with compelling, intriguing, and relevant "discussable" texts. The subject matter of these collections could not be more compelling, intriguing, or urgently relevant to today's students and the world they are poised to inherit. The anthologized articles also provide the basis for stimulating, lively, and passionate classroom debates. Students who are compelled to anticipate objections to their own argument and identify the flaws in those of an opponent read more carefully, think more critically, and steep themselves in relevant context, facts, and information more thoroughly. In short, using discussable text of the kind provided by every single volume in the Current Controversies series encourages close reading, facilitates reading comprehension, fosters research, strengthens critical thinking, and greatly enlivens and energizes classroom discussion and participation. The entire learning process is deepened, extended, and strengthened.

If we are to foster a knowledgeable, responsible, active, and engaged citizenry, we must provide readers with the intellectual, interpretive, and critical-thinking tools and experience necessary to make sense of the world around them and of the all-important debates and arguments that inform it. We must encourage them not to run away from or attempt to quell controversy but to embrace it in a responsible, conscientious, and thoughtful way, to sharpen and strengthen their own informed opinions by listening to and critically analyzing those of others. This series encourages respectful engagement with and analysis of current controversies and competing opinions and fosters a resulting increase in the strength and rigor of one's own opinions and stances. As such, it helps readers assume their rightful place in the public square and provides them with the skills necessary to uphold their awesome responsibility—guaranteeing the continued and future health of a vital, vibrant, and free democracy.

Introduction

> *"The world is neither unipolar,*
> *multipolar, nor chaotic—it is all*
> *three at the same time."*
>
> —Joseph Nye, *"The*
> *Future of Power"*

O ur world runs on relationships between states. It is these relationships that dictate trade, travel, growth, and the exchange of knowledge. These relationships also dictate war and conflict, and the ways in which we respond to unrest. For most of human history, diplomacy—the practice of negotiation between states—and war have been the primary tools a state or government could exercise to build relationships. But in the twentieth century, a new, globalized world order started to emerge, and with it a new, informal way of conducting relationships.

In his 1990 book *Bound to Lead: The Changing Nature of American Power*, the political scientist Joseph Nye coined a new term: "soft power." The world was changing rapidly, and with it the nature of diplomacy. Nye saw that old ways of influencing foreign affairs were still effective but were only part of the puzzle. Soft power, he argued, was a form of influence tied to culture and the ways in which a given country appeared to the world. Through sports, media, food, or the arts, a country could build relationships on an individual level with foreign populations, which would in turn make the governments of those foreign countries more open to negotiating or building alliances.

Since 1990, countries around the world have worked to understand how soft power fits into the larger landscape of international relations. Diplomacy and military action—sometimes called hard power—have been used for centuries to build trust, cooperation, and relationships between governments. But soft power is something different. It can't be directly controlled, since it relies on how one country's culture spreads in a different country, where it can be adapted or understood in different ways. Soft power also doesn't provide concrete gains in terms of what we think of as power; it's hard to quantify the influence popular American music has had on building relationships between the United States and Germany, for example.

Since the mid-twentieth century, culture has been a tool used by states to gain influence, most notably the United States. During the Cold War (1947-1991), the United States promoted democracy as being represented by American products like Hershey's chocolate bars and denim jeans, which became popular behind the Iron Curtain. In the 1970s, the United States and China hosted table tennis tournaments to encourage cross-cultural exchange, calling the events "ping-pong diplomacy." But globalization has accelerated the speed with which culture spreads. Today, states have less control over what pieces of their culture are shared with the world or how they are adopted and interpreted. Social media in particular has created opportunities for leadership from around the world to interact with citizens, for music or movies to be accessed almost anywhere, and for citizens to build relationships with one another without even leaving their homes. Our world, and the way we interact with it, is rapidly changing.

Experts do agree that soft power, particularly in the age of social media, has a role to play in how we strategize and understand international relations. But how it fits into diplomacy and how it can be used alongside hard power—which includes both military action and the threat of military action—is less clear. Without tangible ways of understanding or guiding the influence gained by soft power, some feel it is an inadequate tool that needs to be used sparingly, while others argue that in today's globalized world, war is too risky to be sustainable, making soft power preferable.

Similarly, some feel that certain states, including those that are actively hostile, simply cannot be reached with soft power and diplomacy, making military intervention the only viable choice in the face of confrontation. There are also disagreements about whether soft power upholds strong states while making it difficult for smaller states to gain influence, which would make soft power less democratic than some have claimed it to be.

This volume explores the complex ways in which diplomacy, soft power, and hard power interact with and strengthen one another, while also paying close attention to the ways in which all three can post disadvantages when used incorrectly. Readers will be exposed to viewpoints from experts, scholars, practitioners, and leaders on how soft power and diplomacy function and on how relationships between states continue to grow and evolve in the twenty-first century.

Does Soft Power Positively Influence International Affairs?

Public Diplomacy Is Changing the Nature of International Relations

Jan Melissen

Jan Melissen is an academic, researcher, and author. He is a senior research fellow at the Clingendael Institute in the Netherlands and a senior fellow in international relations and diplomacy at the Institute of Security and Global Affairs at Leiden University.

[...]

I t is tempting to see public diplomacy as old wine in new bottles. Official communication aimed at foreign publics is after all no new phenomenon in international relations. Image cultivation, propaganda and activities that we would now label as public diplomacy are nearly as old as diplomacy itself. Even in ancient times, prestige-conscious princes and their representatives never completely ignored the potential and pitfalls of public opinion in foreign lands. References to the nation and its image go as far back as the Bible, and international relations in ancient Greece and Rome, Byzantium and the Italian Renaissance were familiar with diplomatic activity aimed at foreign publics.

It was not until the invention of the printing press in the fifteenth century that the scale of official communication with foreign publics potentially altered. Towards the end of the Middle Ages, the Venetians had already introduced the systematic dissemination of newsletters inside their own diplomatic service, but it was Gutenberg's invention that cleared the way for true pioneers in international public relations, such as Cardinal Richelieu in early seventeenth-century France. Under the *ancien régime*, the French went to much greater lengths in remoulding their country's image abroad than other European powers, and they put enormous effort into managing their country's reputation, seeing it as one of the

Jan Melissen, "The New Public Diplomacy. Soft Power in International Relations," by Jan Melissen, Palgrave Macmillan, 2005. Reproduced with permission of SNCSC.

principal sources of a nation's power.[1] Identity creation and image projection—nation-branding in today's parlance—reached a peak under Louis XIV.[2] Other countries followed suit, such as Turkey in the aftermath of the Ottoman Empire. Kemal Atatürk was in charge of nothing less than a complete makeover of the face of his country and its identity, without which Turkey's present prospects of integration into Europe would not have been on the EU's political agenda. Less benign twentieth-century versions of identity development and nation-building—such as Fascism and Communism—directly challenged and gave an impetus towards communication with foreign publics by democratic powers. Political leaders' battles for overseas "hearts and minds" are therefore anything but a recent invention.

The First World War saw the birth of professional image cultivation across national borders, and it was inevitable after the war that the emerging academic study of international politics would wake up to the importance of what is now commonly dubbed as "soft power."[3] In the era of growing inter-state conflict between the two world wars, E. H. Carr wrote that "power over opinion" was "not less essential for political purposes than military and economic power, and has always been closely associated with them." In other words, to put it in the terminology recently introduced by Joseph S. Nye, "hard power" and "soft power" are inextricably linked.[4] It is now a cliché to state that soft power—the postmodern variant of power over opinion—is increasingly important in the global information age, and that in an environment with multiple transnational linkages the loss of soft power can be costly for hard power. Many practical questions about the power of attraction in international affairs are, however, still unanswered. Political commentators in many countries have become gripped by the notion of soft power and ministries of foreign affairs wonder how to wield it most effectively. As Nye argued, countries that are likely to be more attractive in postmodern international relations are those that help to frame issues, whose culture and ideas are closer to prevailing international norms, and whose credibility abroad is reinforced by their values and policies.[5]

Public diplomacy is one of soft power's key instruments, and this was recognized in diplomatic practice long before the contemporary debate on public diplomacy. The United States, the former Soviet Union and Europe's three major powers invested particularly heavily in their "communications with the world" during the Cold War. Although conventional diplomatic activity and public diplomacy were mostly pursued on parallel tracks, it became increasingly hard to see how the former could be effective without giving sufficient attention to the latter.[6] In fact, as early as 1917–18, Wilson and Lenin had already challenged one another at the soft power level, long before their countries turned into global superpowers and started colliding in the military and economic fields.[7] The battle of values and ideas that dominated international relations in the second half of the twentieth century evolved into competition in the sphere of hard power, and not vice versa. The world diplomatic community nevertheless woke up late to the fundamental challenges of communication with foreign publics rather than then habitual international dialogue with foreign officials. Diplomatic culture is after all fundamentally peer-orientated, and the dominant realist paradigm in diplomatic circles was a by-product of a long history of viewing international relations in terms of economic and military power. The question today of how foreign ministries can instrumentalize soft power is testing their diplomats' flexibility to the full.

Against this backdrop it may not be surprising to see that most students of diplomacy have given little systematic attention to public diplomacy. The basic distinction between traditional diplomacy and public diplomacy is clear: the former is about relationships between the representatives of states, or other international actors; whereas the latter targets the general public in foreign societies and more specific non-official groups, organizations and individuals. Existing definitions of diplomacy have either stressed its main purpose ("the art of resolving international difficulties peacefully"), its principal agents ("the conduct of relations between sovereign states through the medium of accredited representatives") or its chief function ("the management of international relations by negotiation"). In a sense, such definitions do not take into account the transformation of the environment in which diplomacy is at work. Students of diplomacy saw diplomatic communication in principle as an activity between symmetrical actors. A more inclusive view of diplomacy as "the mechanism of representation, communication and negotiation through which states and other international actors conduct their business" still suggests a neat international environment consisting of a range of clearly identifiable players.[8]

Diplomacy in a traditionalist view is depicted as a game where the roles and responsibilities of actors in international relations are clearly delineated. This picture no longer resembles the much more fuzzy world of postmodern transnational relations—a world, for that matter, in which most actors are not nearly as much in control as they would like to be. Moreover, the interlocutors of today's foreign service officers are not necessarily their counterparts, but a wide variety of people that are either involved in diplomatic activity or are at the receiving end of international politics. As a result, the requirements of diplomacy have been transformed. As Robert Cooper put it, success in diplomacy "means openness and transnational cooperation."[9] Such openness and multi-level cooperation call for the active pursuit of more collaborative diplomatic relations with various types of actors. Public diplomacy is an indispensable ingredient for such a collaborative model of diplomacy.[10]

[...]

Notes

1. Michael Kunczik, "Transnational Public Relations by Foreign Governments," Sriramesh, Krishnamurthy and Dejan Vercic (eds), *The Global Public Relations Handbook: Theory, Research and Practice* (Mahwah NJ and London: Lawrence Erlbaum Associates, 2003), pp. 399–405. On France and nation-branding, see the chapter in this book by Wally Olins.

2. On nation-branding, see Wally Olins' chapter in this book and *Wally Olins on Brand* (London: Thames & Hudson, 2003).

3. See, for instance, Joseph S. Nye, "Soft Power," *Foreign Policy*, no. 80, autumn 1990; Joseph S. Nye and William A. Owens, "America's Information Edge," *Foreign Affairs*, vol. 75, no. 2, March/April 1996; and, for a recent elaboration of this concept, see Joseph S. Nye, *Soft Power: The Means to Success in World Politics* (New York: Public Affairs, 2004).

4. E. H. Carr, *The Twenty Years' Crisis 1919–1939: An Introduction to the Study of International Relations* (Basingstoke: Macmillan, 1983 (first edn 1939)), pp. 132 and 141.

5. Nye, *Soft Power*, pp. 31 and 32.

6. Hans N. Tuch, *Communicating with the World: US Public Diplomacy Overseas* (New York: St Martin's Press 1990); and Wilson P. Dizard, *Inventing Public Diplomacy: The Story of the US Information Agency* (Boulder CO and London: Lynne Rienner, 2004).

7. Arno J. Mayer, *Political Origins of the New Diplomacy 1917–1918* (New York: Vintage Books, 1970).

8. Jan Melissen (ed.), *Innovation in Diplomatic Practice* (Basingstoke: Macmillan, 1999), pp. xvi–xvii.

9. Robert Cooper, *The Breaking of Nations: Order and Chaos in the Twenty-First Century* (London: Atlantic Books, 2003), p. 76.

10. Shaun Riordan, *The New Diplomacy* (London: Polity, 2003), especially ch. 9.

Soft Power Strengthens Emerging States

Francesca Centracchio

Francesca Centracchio is a journalist and writer whose work focuses on politics.

Brazil is being referred to as an emerging world power more frequently as we move into the 21st century. Its economy has risen to be in the top ten internationally and Brazil has started to make a name for itself on the international stage. A unique aspect of Brazil's rise is its abundance of *soft power*. Soft power is defined as a persuasive approach to international relations, in which a country uses its economy or cultural influence to motivate other countries to cooperate. This is in contrast to hard power which is the use of force or threats of potential force. Brazil is one of the few rising powers with a lack of hard power; however they have managed to stay relevant through their soft power.

Brazil has always been influential throughout South America because of its territorial size, wealth of resources, economy and large population. Brazil also has a western view on the world that has aligned them with the US since the Second World War, when Brazil sent troops to Europe in an agreement with the US for support in development. Up until the end of the 1970s the United States was concerned with maintaining relations with Brazil as a strong hold in South America. Brazil became more independent throughout the 1980s when the country had a debt crisis and threatened not to pay back its debtors, which included the US. However, by 1985 Brazil started to turn around with its new democratic government. The democratic government has provided political stability for Brazil.

"Brazil's Soft Power As a Tool for World Power Emerging Process," by Francesca Centracchio, Center for International Studies, January 18, 2016, https://cesi-italia.org/en/articoli/506/brazils-soft-power-as-a-tool-for-world-power-emerging-process. Licensed under CC BY-SA 3.0.

Unlike many other emerging powers, Brazil seems to have few to no enemies. Within South America they have no territorial disputes or rivals. Much of this is due to the countries approach to international relations. In Article 4 of the Federal constitution the guidelines are set for how Brazil should approach other countries, which is non-intervention, self-determination, international cooperation and the peaceful settlement of conflicts. Brazil learned a lot from its early dealings with America and how it intervened in their country like many others. From being on the other side of a super power, Brazil has taken the opposite approach most likely because they know how it feels to be the "inferior" country. Instead of force, Brazil sets its personal agenda through helping its neighbors and trying to find ways to benefit both of them.

One way that Brazil builds strong relationships with other South American countries is by having Brazilian political strategists assist candidates in other countries in their campaigns. They will back a candidate and then use the success of Brazilian democracy to help a foreign candidate appeal to a larger constituency. This has worked with presidents and politicians of Peru, Venezuela, El Salvador and Paraguay. By establishing a strong connection with the leader, Brazil can then start to work with the other countries to expand business, infrastructure and overall its influence in the region. The consultants have also been able to help moderate some of the more extremist South American leaders and shift the focus to the voters. Leadership has shifted from the US to Brazil now when it comes to who Latin America looks to follow.

Brazil has also strengthened its relations in South America through trade organizations, and has pointedly left out the US in some of these organizations. Brazil is not afraid to step out from under American policy after years of American agenda setting. Now that Brazil feels comfortable within its own continent it has started to become a larger player in international relations. One way Brazil has gotten involved internationally is through joining many organizations such as BRICS (Brazil, Russia, India, China, and South Africa), G-15, G-20, G-24, G-5, G-77 international groups.

BRICS is an economic organization that links the main emerging powers in the World. The members all have large economies and are advanced countries, but they have often been left out when it comes to major international decisions in the past. Each of the other groups listed above have their own specific purpose like industrial countries, developing countries, etc. These groups help expand Brazil's economy and soft power to other parts of the World.

Within the last year, Brazil has truly proven that its soft power and lack of enemies gives it a unique edge in negotiating. Iran and Brazil have continued to have relations even after sanctions were placed on Iran because of its nuclear program. During nuclear agreement talks this past year Brazil placed itself in the middle of the conversation and worked with both sides. Not many countries are able to say that they could peacefully talk with the US one minute then switch and be friendly with Iran without deeply offending both sides. The President of Iran posted on his website that Iran would like Brazil to mediate during the deal, making it impossible for Brazil to be left by the way side like in the past. Brazil had slightly more relaxed views to how to handle Iran than other western countries, they were willing to work with both sides but said that everyone would need to be flexible in the talks. While Russia, Germany, Britain, France, China, and the US were the main players in the deal, Brazil came one step closer to earning a seat at the major world powers table. However, Brazil has used agreeability and peaceful persuasion to get there instead of force and sheer power like many of the current powers.

While Brazil's soft power has gotten it this far it is unclear whether this is enough to push it up to the next level. Not only does the country have to break through the barriers that keep the US and western European countries at the top, but Brazil is also competing with the other emerging powers to be at the top. China and Russia among those powers already have permanent seats on the UN Security Council, and they also have significant hard power to back up their decisions. Another difference is that Russia, China, and India all have nuclear power and while it is not used the threat of them having that gives them significant power. The US knows that it will need to be on good terms with Brazil since it is a regional power in South America, but without the fear that Brazil will retaliate if America does not give into Brazil's wants.

Soft power will continue to become more and more important on the world stage to prevent conflicts before they happen. In addition, soft power can help reduce the use of hard power and create a more hegemonic international community. This doesn't mean that Brazil has what it takes to be the next major superpower though. It will be hard for Brazil to be taken seriously if it cannot use force like other powers. For instance, the US doesn't fear that Brazil will throw a temper tantrum if they aren't given what they want unlike China who will take measures to punish the US. Brazil will keep itself in the middle of international relations through its ability to get along with all, but in today's political culture it seems that a country needs to spark a little bit of fear into other countries in order to be seen as a power house. There is no way to know for sure that Brazil won't become a main power, but at this point unless they can be the only country to be able to solve a conflict or are viewed as absolutely vital to the other powers, the country will probably stay at the same power level it is now, just below the main powers.

Soft Power Has Real Impact Around the World

David Ensor

David Ensor is the director of the Project for Media and National Security at George Washington University.

In August 2014, ISIS attacks the town of Shinjar in northern Iraq, sending hundreds of thousands of members of the ancient religious minority known as the Yazidis fleeing up onto Mount Shinjar. Those not already captured are quickly surrounded. Information is scarce, but Voice of America's Kurdish Service has a Yazidi reporter who soon hears from his people—with what is left of the power in their cell phones.

Hundreds of children are dying on the mountain, they tell him. There is no shelter, no food or water. Many have already been executed. Hundreds of young women are being held, raped and used as sex slaves. VOA's exclusive details are picked up by regional media, alerting US policymakers.

"I was talking with one of the ladies, for example," says Iraqi-born journalist Dakhil Elias. "She was captured with fifteen hundred other women and children held prisoner in a school building. She was telling me: 'Please bomb us! We want to die, not to stay here under ISIS.'"[1] VOA's Elias is invited to two White House meetings with the president's deputy national security advisor, where he shares some of the harrowing testimony.

Within days, the US airdrops humanitarian aid on the mountain and then targets airstrikes against ISIS positions around it. The offensive allows Kurdish forces to reach the mountain and lift the siege.

The story of the encircled Yazidis underscores what key policymakers in the White House and State Department know well: the Voice of America (VOA) is a national security asset, and not only because it is a news organization of extraordinary breadth, depth and reach. Many of its best journalists hail from places such as China and Tibet, the Russian Caucasus, northern Nigeria, Venezuela, Iraq or Iran. They are indispensable experts.

Funded by the US government, VOA is by law an editorially independent media organization. With an annual budget of $212 million, VOA has a weekly international audience of almost 188 million people; an increase of 40 percent in the past four years despite budget reductions in real terms each of those years.[2] It reaches them in more than 45 languages through television, radio, Internet and social media—and does so whether their governments like it or not.

VOA is an effort to harness and direct the nation's soft power by exporting truthful, balanced journalism. This is a model of state broadcasting with a long history, credited with contributing to the peaceful demise of the Soviet Union.

There are influential voices in Washington, however, calling for change. They would make VOA a full-throated advocate for American policy. Their argument is that in the digital age, when there are hundreds of voices out there, everyone is going to have to "spin" in order to have real impact. The traditional model of journalism in the service of objectivity and balance is, they say, outdated. They repeatedly press to change VOA's mission.

The US International Communications Reform Act of 2014 proposed by Chairman Ed Royce (R-Calif) of the House Committee on Foreign Affairs would have required VOA to "promote" the foreign policy objectives[3] of the administration in power. While the House of Representatives passed the bill with bipartisan support, it expired at the end of the congressional session without Senate action.

Royce has a new version (HR 2323), introduced in this Congress, which seeks to reduce VOA from the full-service news organization it is now, to one which exclusively reports on US related news. The bill would also create duplication and exacerbate an already unhealthy rivalry with three smaller sister US broadcasting entities, by putting them under a different governing and oversight structure.

In 2013, a former senior official in the Bush administration went still further, arguing in congressional testimony that the VOA and its parent agency "should be part of the State Department" and that it "should not be in the journalism business but in the foreign policy business."[4]

James Glassman, a former undersecretary of state and former chairman of the Broadcasting Board of Governors (BBG), the parent agency of VOA, believes that the BBG has two incompatible goals: "Its mission is contradictory and confused. The law asks it both to be a tool of US foreign policy and an independent, unbiased journalistic organization, protected from government interference."[5] Instead, Glassman argued, the "mission should be the same as that of the State Department itself: to achieve the specific goals of US national security and foreign policy."[6]

At a July 2015 management retreat a senior official at the BBG proposed reshaping and redirecting the work of VOA and its sister organizations under the policy goal of "countering violent extremism." A number of VOA journalists argued such a move would break down the "firewall" between journalism and policy, damaging VOA's credibility. The proposal was quietly shelved but continues to have influential supporters in Congress and the bureaucracy.

The West today faces information challenges from the likes of Russia's global TV broadcaster RT, China's CCTV and Iran's Press TV, not to mention the need to combat Internet recruitment drives by terrorist groups. The age of global satellite channels and digital media is reshaping the media landscape, creating extraordinary new challenges and opportunities. Yet rather than focusing fully on how to respond to those challenges and take advantage of the digital communications revolution, Washington has instead been cutting budgets and rehashing an old debate about VOA's mission.

What is the proper role of the Voice of America in a world where Vladimir Putin "weaponizes information"[7] and terrorists recruit globally on the Internet?

In today's media environment, are state broadcasters that advocate for their governments delivering larger audiences and greater impact than those that work to report the news as objectively as possible?

In the digital age, should VOA become a policy-driven advocacy voice? Or, should VOA continue to offer balanced, truthful journalism? And if the choice is journalism, how can we make it more effective?

These are the important questions this paper seeks to address.

Soft Power

Funding international media is just one of many tools at the disposal of governments to attract and persuade foreign publics and governments. Harvard professor Joseph Nye, who coined the term "soft power" in 1990, says the need to understand and use it effectively is only growing. "In this confused, complex multipolar world, the limits of hard power—the use of force, threats, sanctions or payments—are becoming more obvious."[8]

The sources of American soft power range from Hollywood to Harvard, from the Bill & Melinda Gates Foundation to Apple, Facebook and Twitter. Also on the list are the US Bill of Rights, and America's reputation as a nation of immigrants. On the other side of the balance sheet are aspects of American life or policy that repel foreign publics, such as too many guns on our streets, and a perception that the US wages too many wars. Portland Communications, a British consulting firm, recently designed a tool to measure and evaluate a nation's soft power. In 2015, it published the "Soft Power 30" report, a list of the nations that wield the greatest soft power. Britain wins. America comes third. China is 30th, and Russia does not make the list.[9]

Many of the efforts by the US government to harness American soft power and persuade global audiences to follow this country's lead are run by the State Department under the heading of Public Diplomacy. Richard Stengel, the current undersecretary of state for public diplomacy, has focused much of his attention on countering terrorists' recruiting messages online. With a budget of just $5.8 million,[10] the State Department's Center for Strategic Counterterrorism Communications (CSCC) works through websites and online chat rooms, collaborating with partners in the Arab World such as the Sawab Center in the UAE.

"We have a campaign," Stengel says, "which is using direct testimony from dozens and dozens of young men and women who have come back from Iraq and Syria and said the Caliphate is a myth. You know, 'I was abused there. They're not religious. They're venal and money-grubbing.' So that type of campaign to refute their disinformation is the kind of thing that we're doing."[11]

Journalism as US Soft Power

VOA was founded in 1942, using a borrowed British transmitter to broadcast shortwave radio programming in German. The founding concept was taken from the BBC. On the first broadcast, it was said: "The news may be good for us. The news may be bad. But we will tell you the truth."[12]

The signature of President Gerald Ford in 1976 on the VOA Charter codified that promise into law. Sponsored by Senator Charles Percy (R-Ill) and Representative Bella Abzug (D-NY), it was passed after battles with the Nixon White House over what VOA could say on the air about the Vietnam War and the Watergate scandal.

The charter requires VOA journalism to be "reliable and authoritative," and to report news that is "accurate, objective and comprehensive." It also requires that VOA "present the policies of the United States clearly and effectively" and present "responsible discussion and opinion on these policies."[13]

Rather than advocating for the policies of the current administration, the concept is to seek credibility with coverage that is honest about America's own debates and controversies, and to present all sides of the argument. Thus VOA reported fully on stories like the revelations of Edward Snowden about NSA surveillance, and on the protests in Ferguson, Missouri and other cities against police killings of young African Americans. It also televised—live to Iran, with Farsi translation—Israeli Prime Minister Benjamin Netanyahu's speech before the US Congress against the Iran nuclear deal, even though he was attacking a key aspect of President Obama's foreign policy.

Given the existence of CNN and other international news channels, some ask what is the need for a VOA? The answer is that commercial broadcasters run on the profit motive. There is little profit in international broadcasts in Farsi, Mandarin, Hausa, Bambara or for that matter English programming designed specifically for key African audiences. But US national interests are served by targeting audiences in parts of the world where reliable news is hard to find, or where information about US policy is often served up with a strong anti-American tilt. VOA news programs and websites delivered in multiple languages deepen international understanding of American policies and values and hence promote freedom of speech and democracy. Also, VOA journalists can make news judgements independent of market considerations. If a dozen new health clinics open in Afghanistan, for example, that is news Afghans want to know about, just as much as the last Taliban attack. Commercial media are sometimes accused—not always fairly—of an "if it bleeds it leads" approach, which is far from the way non-commercial VOA makes its coverage decisions.

The US is one of relatively few nations on earth not to have a state broadcaster on the air domestically. As a result, few Americans—and few of their elected representatives—know that VOA is one of the world's largest, most influential media organizations. They are more likely to know about the even bigger British broadcaster that it was designed to emulate.

[...]

Endnotes

1. The author conducted an interview with Dakhil Elias, Voice of America Kurdish Service journalist, on September 14, 2015, via video conference.

2. Broadcasting Board of Governors, "2015 Performance and Accountability Report," October 2015. http://www.bbg.gov/wp-content/media/2015/11/BBG-FY2015 -PAR.pdf

3. The full text of H.R. 4490 United States International Communications Reform Act of 2014 can be found on the website of the US House Committee on Foreign Affairs: https://foreignaffairs.house.gov/bill/hr-united-states-international -communications-reform-act-2014

4. The full transcript of the testimony of James K. Glassman, founding executive director of the George W. Bush Institute, to the US House Committee on Foreign Affairs Committee's June 26, 2013 hearing on "The Broadcasting Board of Governors: An Agency Defunct" can be found on the website of the Committee: http://docs.house.gov/meetings/FA/FA00/20130626/101050/HHRG-113-FA00 -Wstate-GlassmanJ-20130626.pdf

5. Ibid.

6. Ibid.

7. The author conducted an interview with Peter Pomerantsev, Legatum Institute, on October 7, 2015, via video conference.

8. Portland Communications, "Soft Power 30," July 2015, p. 7. http://sp.portlandvault .com/ranking/#2015

9. Ibid. p. 18.

10. US Department of State, "Foreign Operations and Related Programs: Budget Amendment Justification, Fiscal Year 2015," 2015. http://www.state.gov /documents/organization/234238.pdf

11. Voice of America, "Interview with US Under Secretary of State for Public Diplomacy and Public Affairs Richard Stengel," September 25, 2015. http://www .state.gov/documents/organization/234238.pdf

12. Heil, Alan L. Jr., *Voice of America: A History* (New York: Columbia University Press, 2003), p. 57.

13. Voice of America Charter, Section 3, 1976. http://www.insidevoa.com/p/5728 .html

Soft Power Cannot Counter Hard Power in International Relations

Michael Cecire

Michael Cecire is a policy researcher whose work focuses on Eurasia and international development.

The Russian invasion of Ukraine has already punctured much of the prevailing foreign-policy thinking that had become pro forma in Washington and Europe. In particular, the notion that Western unilateral disarmament can somehow be balanced or compensated for with less tangible forms of influence—soft power—has much to answer for in this ongoing crisis. By now, it is clear that Moscow's actions in Crimea strongly demonstrate the sharp limits of soft power, especially one that appears to have been decoupled from hard power, the traditional final arbiter of interstate relations. Ukraine is not merely a geopolitical setback, but a symptom of a misplaced faith in the potency of postmodern soft power as foreign policy plan A through Z.

Ukraine's rapid transformation from *homo Sovieticus*–ruled kleptocracy to inspiring popular revolution to the latest victim of Russian imperialism has been astonishing. In the span of mere weeks, Ukraine's political cleavages have been magnified as the faultline of a tense geopolitical contest between the Euro-Atlantic community and a revanchist, increasingly militant Russia. In the Western scramble to come to terms with the new threat landscape— let alone formulating an effective, unified response—Crimea has almost certainly already been lost . Meanwhile, Russia seems poised to expand its writ into other areas of eastern Ukraine just as it aggressively probes Euro-Atlantic readiness in the Baltic, Turkey, and the Caucasus. In Washington, defense and administration officials appear resigned—if only unofficially—to Russian control

"The Limits of Soft Power," by Michael Cecire, Center for the National Interest, April 1, 2014. Reprinted by permission.

over Crimea (if not eastern Ukraine) and are digging in for the long haul.

How did we get here? Among the ideologues, the answer lies in the foreign policies of the current or previous administrations. On the right, President Obama's "reset" and subordination of foreign policy to domestic issues is the obvious cause. And on the left, President Bush's wars have given the Kremlin the perfect moral justification. But the reality, like many things, is hardly one sided. Partisans decrying President Obama's "weakness" appear to ignore that the administration's response to Russia's occupation of Crimea is already far more muscular than President Bush's reaction to the Russian invasion of Georgia 2008. And conversely, some of the left's bizarre use of a war they supposedly opposed to equivocate on the invasion of a sovereign state by corrupt autocracy is as self-contradictory as it is troubling.

The likelier culprit is not so intimately tethered to the tribalisms of American politics, though ideology inevitably has played a role. Instead, the Western political class has become intoxicated with the notion that soft power, now the highly fashionable foreign-policy instrument of first resort, can compensate for—or in some ways replace altogether—diminished hard power. If the late 1990s was the heyday for liberal internationalism by airpower, the late 2000s saw an analogous consensus congregate around soft power.

Soft power is supposed to describe the latent factors—values, economy, culture and the like—of a state, entity or idea to persuade or attract. This contrasts with its more recognizable counterpart, hard power, which is based on the more traditional principle of coercion. There is little doubt that soft power is a real and fundamentally important phenomenon in the conduct of international relations. Contributions from scholars like Joseph Nye and Giulio Gallarotti have made a compelling case that soft power is a powerful geopolitical signifier; but what began as a keen observation had morphed into a cottage industry looking to leverage soft power into a foreign-policy panacea.

In an illuminating 2011 paper published by the Strategic Studies Institute at the US Army War College, University of Reading (U.K.) political scientist Colin S. Gray rightly acknowledges the merits of the soft-power thesis while articulating its practical limitations, particularly in the policy arena.

"While it is sensible to seek influence abroad as cost-effectively as possible, it is only prudent to be modest in one's expectations of the soft power to be secured by cultural influence," cautions Gray. Indeed, soft power's attraction and subsequent embrace by the foreign policy elite had as much to do with its usefulness as a substitute for "hard power" as its salience as an idea. But while hard and soft power can be complementary, Gray observes that soft power can in no way compensate for military power. "Sad to say," laments Gray, "there is no convincing evidence suggesting an absence of demand for the threat and use of military force." Sad, indeed.

However, events in Ukraine have exposed the stark limits of soft power in a way that no analysis ever could. There is no small irony in the fact that Russia's forceful military intervention into Ukraine was preceded by a grinding, if superficially velveted, tug of war between Moscow and the West over Ukraine's integration with two competing soft-power "vehicles"—the EU and the Moscow-led Customs Union-cum-Eurasian Union. It was Yanukovych's abandonment of Ukraine's pledge to sign an Association Agreement with the EU—following intense Russian coercion—that protests began again in earnest. Yanukovych's turn to brutality eventually precipitated his toppling, Russia's military intervention, and now Crimea's annexation.

The idea of soft power as operational policy should be buried. While there is some government role in propagating and wielding soft power—public affairs, policy making, and, yes, sometimes psychological operations—the real business of soft power exists well outside of the domain of the state. In reality, the track record of operationalizing soft power has been, to date, abysmal. Russia is a case in point. Moscow repeatedly sought to revise the post–Cold War order through a variety of projects that might normally be filed as soft-power initiatives: then president Dmitry Medvedev's repeated attempts to reorient the European security architecture; the Kremlin obsession with making the ruble an international reserve currency; the formation of the Russia-led Customs Union in 2010; and the (now likely stillborn) plans to establish the Eurasian Union. And yet, in the end, Crimea was forcibly seized by men with guns.

Indeed, the truer currency of power remains the ability to coerce. Fatigue from disastrous wars in Iraq and Afghanistan elevated expectations that soft power could supplant a beleaguered and overstretched US military. Why, indeed, would the US opt for coercion when civilizational persuasion could do the trick? Pro-West people power in Eurasia seemed to bolster the case for operationalized soft power after the "color revolutions" in Georgia, Ukraine and Kyrgyzstan. Yet the longer-term results were unpredictable at best and disastrous at worst. Over time, it has become increasingly apparent that soft power is perhaps less an instrument to wield than a favorable wind at our backs.

The crisis with Russia has laid bare the limits of soft power as well as the continued relevance of hard power—even in "postmodern" Europe. While the Obama administration should be credited with being among the few Western governments to offer a relatively serious response to the Ukraine crisis, the White House overall still seems uncomfortable with the difficult but very real role that hard power necessarily plays in establishing and policing a US-led, liberal normative order. This must change with the new circumstances established by Russian revanchism. Western values can only be propagated and upheld with the ultimate guarantee of hard power. And if the West is not prepared to enforce its values with tangible consequences, then perhaps we should abandon the pretense of a rules-based international system and cease the cruel practice of giving hope where there is none to be had.

Soft power is here to stay, but its moment as a diplomatic instrument has long since gone. Because, in reality, it was never really much more than an illusion of what we wished the world to be rather than the one that exists.

There Is No Evidence Culture Shapes International Affairs

Deborah Bull

Baroness Deborah Bull is the vice president and vice principal of King's College London.

In January 2015, I attended the World Economic Forum in Davos where I spoke about the impact of arts and culture on some of our global challenges—across society, the economy, education, health and wellbeing. In the questions that followed, I was asked whether there was equivalent evidence for the use of culture in the service of soft power. Having looked at a wide range of research to prepare for my speech I could confirm, unequivocally, that there is not.

Over recent years, soft power has gained a significant reputation and, in some countries, substantial government investment. This is despite the absence of a body of research that would prove the efficacy of art in soft power. Those people working in arts education or in the area of arts and health can draw upon robust research to make their case and to make effective choices around how scarce resources are allocated. There simply isn't the same kind of evidence available to people working in the field of cultural diplomacy. Given the enormous claims made for the role of culture in diplomacy—and the drive towards evidence-led policy—it's surprising that this particular contribution of the cultural sector has remained out of the critical gaze of academic scrutiny: poorly articulated and poorly understood.

This may be an apposite time to attempt to increase our understanding of soft power's potential: as the world-order undergoes significant change and long-held international alliances

"The Art of Soft Power: A Study Of Cultural Diplomacy," by Deborah Bull, Vice President & Vice Principal (London), King's College London, November 13, 2017. Reprinted by permission.

shift and evolve, the kind of diplomacy that operates outside the formal channels of hard edged politics is likely to become increasingly important.

My interlocutor at Davos turned out to be Lithuania's Ambassador to the United Nations Office at Geneva (UNOG), Rytis Paulauskas. In follow up conversations, Rytis suggested that UNOG—a microcosm of world politics in which communities of diplomats seek to influence one another not only through formal sessions but through a structured Cultural Activities Programme —might offer a unique laboratory for investigating the ways in which culture is deployed in the service of diplomacy.

The contained environment of UNOG had immediate appeal. The study of soft power is fraught with practical problems. It's easy to measure how many people saw a piece of art: much harder to measure whether (and how) it changed their feelings towards the country that presented it—particularly when that change may take place in different ways, in different circumstances and, often, years down the line.

Another significant challenge is the absence of a shared understanding of what soft power (or cultural diplomacy) really means—the terms are used interchangeably (and, by some people, consciously avoided). There is, of course, Joseph Nye's famous starting point—the ability to attract and persuade—but our research in Geneva uncovered over 150 responses to a question about how soft power is articulated, understood and practiced.

It's also true that cultural diplomacy has something of a shadowy reputation and may even be most effective when government involvement is at a distance, out of sight. A report by Christopher Hill and Susan Beadle for the British Academy in 2014 urged caution for scholars seeking to measure, understand or account for soft power, and for governments seeking to deploy it. They argued that when governments conspicuously use soft power (in national branding campaigns, for example) it frequently backfires. None of us wants to feel that our feelings are being targeted in order that they can be at best influenced or, at worst, manipulated—and we certainly don't want governments doing the manipulating. So soft power is, if you like, the ninja of the cultural policy world. It operates by stealth. This presents a challenge to anyone wanting to study the ways in which it works.

Researching the processes and effects of soft power among a community like UNOG may present its own challenges. In a multilateral environment, sophisticated diplomats attempt to influence the thoughts, feelings and behaviours of fellow sophisticated diplomats—professionals whose skill-set includes the ability to resist (or at least moderate) external influence. This is different from a bilateral setting, where the influencing effort is focussed on people who don't necessarily possess these same attributes.

The research project that followed was based on interviews with 20 diplomats and the UNOG secretariat undertaken during five fieldwork trips to Geneva by Melissa Nisbett and James Doeser. This data—and additional information relating to the Cultural Activities Programme in and around the Palais des Nations, the main UNOG campus—was investigated using Thematic Analysis.

The opportunity to study this distinctive "tribe" in its natural habitat was both rare and revealing. Private spaces and private lives were shown to be important soft power tools and—in contrast to academic assumptions in the existing cultural diplomacy literature—the researchers found a clear connection between cultural spaces and political meaning. The manifold responses of the various interviewees fell into two distinct categories: "reaching out" (cultural diplomacy) and "standing out" (soft power). These dual notions might initially seem to be at odds, but they mirror the blend of leadership and collaboration required in tackling the kinds of global challenges that are the daily business of UNOG.

The experience in Geneva led the researchers to question whether an alternative to the usual starting points of political science, economics or sociology methodologies might prove fruitful in the study of soft power. The rituals, performance and behaviours of the diplomatic tribe—along with the settings, clothing, mannerisms and body language displayed—suggest that looking through an anthropological lens could offer new insights.

In the initial scoping visit to UNOG, I was privileged to take part in early conversations in which diplomats and their officers shared fascinating insights into the ways in which arts and culture create opportunities to develop, enhance and maintain relationships. There were many different perspectives but over and over, the same truth emerged: interviewees expressed an intuitive feeling that "something good" came out of cultural activities, but admitted that they had never stopped to question, explore or articulate this supposed chain of causality.

Over the course of that visit, it dawned on me that I was almost certainly the only person in the conversations who had actually been deployed as a tool of cultural diplomacy. As a dancer with The Royal Ballet I performed in many tours abroad, some of which were at particularly strategic moments in time: China in 1983; Russia in 1987; Australia in 1988 and many more. In 2008 I danced in Beijing again, in the section of the Closing ceremony of the Olympic Games that marked the handover to London, the next host city.

Perhaps the artist in me should be happy to believe that art has the power to change how people feel, think and behave—to accept that "something good" happens, and leave it there. But the analyst in me is not. And besides, if we can evidence what so many of us believe instinctively to be true—that art can build bridges and promote understanding between nations—this might be a very good moment to understand more about the how and the why.

Soft Power Benefits Strong States More than Others

Melissa Nisbett

Melissa Nisbett is an academic at King's College London whose research focuses on culture and power, including how the arts are used in diplomacy.

In a world where global relations are becoming increasingly complex, intercultural understanding has perhaps never been so important. Over the last 10 years, terms such as "soft power" and "cultural diplomacy" have received increasing political attention and have gained traction within governments around the world (for example, in Britain, the United States, Russia, Australia, China, and India). Whether viewed as foreign policy or cultural policy, governments have undoubtedly begun to take the role of culture within international relations more seriously.

There has been some scholarly interest alongside this political engagement. A recent issue of the *International Journal of Cultural Policy* was dedicated to cultural diplomacy. This was encouraging, since despite the subject straddling political science, international relations, and cultural policy studies, there has been remarkably little research. The discussion of instrumentalism within cultural policy studies is well rehearsed and cultural policy making from economic and social angles has been thoroughly explored (see, for example, Belfiore 2002; Gray 2007; Mirza 2006). Yet almost no attention has been paid to the examination of cultural policy from a foreign policy perspective.

This article contributes to filling this gap in the literature. It is based on the textual analysis of a range of policy documents and semi-structured qualitative interviews with government

"Who Holds the Power in Soft Power?" by Melissa Nisbett, March 13, 2016. This essay appeared in the journal of *Arts & International Affairs* in 2016. See https://theartsjournal.net/2016/03/13/nisbett/.

officials, political advisors, arts managers, and cultural practitioners including artists and curators. The data sets were analyzed using thematic analysis (Braun and Clarke 2006), a method derived from grounded theory (Glaser and Strauss 1967; Charmaz 2006). This article starts by defining the key terms neoliberalism, power, cultural diplomacy and soft power, and critiquing the published work, beginning with the problems of the basic terminology and conceptualizations. I will then introduce the British case, to explore how cultural diplomacy and soft power are communicated at a government level. The discussion is then extrapolated to consider these terms and practices in relation to global changes, the spread of neoliberalism and the shifting world order. It ultimately asks: who holds the power in soft power?

[...]

Soft Power

I will spend some time sketching out and discussing the concepts of soft power and power itself, and then briefly turn my attention to the term cultural diplomacy, before moving on to consider the British case in practice. Soft power is a term that was coined by the political scientist Joseph Nye in 1990 to describe the ability of one country to shape the preferences of another, and to do so through attraction and influence, rather than coercion. The concept emerged within the context of the Cold War, during which American art and culture (such as jazz and the avant-garde Abstract Expressionism movement) was funded[1] and exported across the world for global consumption, promoting the values of intellectual freedom and, more broadly, liberal modern democracy, through self-expression and creativity. This was the antithesis of the alternative offered by the communist Soviet Union. Cultural products have continued to be produced in vast quantities and marketed aggressively to the rest of the world. This is the reason why the terms soft power and cultural diplomacy are associated with cultural imperialism and propaganda. This historicity is important in understanding not only where the term soft power came from and how it specifically refers to a particular moment in time, but also in considering its trajectory over the last 25 years. Nye invented the term in response to claims made by academics, commentators, and advisors in the 1980s that the United States had overstretched its resources during the Cold War and that this would lead to a decline in its position within the international system and on the world stage. While his initial formulation was in response to these "declinists," Nye's notion of soft power has changed over the years, which can be observed across a number of his texts (see Nye 1990, 2002, 2004). These shifts are a reflection of the political context of the day. Whilst these changes have prompted critics to argue that Nye's formulation is "maddeningly inconsistent" (Layne 2010:54), there is some sense in having a concept that can accommodate variation in response to the enormous changes across the world stage and within international relations such as globalization, even if this does not make life easy for scholars and their analysis.

What is perhaps more problematic is the poor explication of the term. Nye's conceptualization of soft power was not fully elucidated in 1990 in general terms or in any detail. He was criticized for this and so *Soft Power—The Means to Success in World Politics* (2004) was an attempt to develop the idea more fully. His descriptions and explanations go some way to sketching out the contours of soft power. However, Nye's 2004 text lacks a coherent theoretical framework overall and is seemingly divorced from social and political theory. It fails to offer any serious scholarly rigor or analytic depth. An example is Nye's opening remarks on the concept of power:

> Power is like the weather. Everyone depends on it and talks about it, but few understand it [...] Power is also like love, easier to experience than to define or measure, but no less real for that. The dictionary tells us that power is the capacity to do things (2004:1).

I will not provide a critique of Nye's writing on soft power, as fulsome commentary already exists elsewhere (see, for example, Parmar and Cox 2010). Instead, I will move away from the generalized and mutable concept offered by Nye throughout his texts, and turn to the issue of power itself. Social and political theory offers a far more sophisticated rendering of the concept of power than that offered by Nye.

Power

Power is the capacity to bring about consequences. It is connected to, but distinct from force (a means of coercion, often through physical strength or the threat of violence) and influence (a mechanism of persuasion that requires knowledge, credibility, respect, and trust). In this article, I refer to the work of the political sociologist Steven Lukes, in thinking further about the notion of power. Lukes claims that there are three dimensions of power. The first is explicit and unconcealed. It takes a prominent role in public decision-making, and manifests in a person or group having power over another or others. One decision or person prevails over another. This idea was put forward by the political theorist Robert Dahl in his seminal book *Who Governs? Democracy and Power in an American City* (1961). It followed the work of the American sociologist C. Wright Mills (1956), who noted that particular individuals occupied particular positions of power within social, economic, and political institutions across America, and thus formed a "power elite."

The second dimension is covert power. This is not just about who or what group prevails, but who controls the agenda on which decisions are based or made. So this is not just about who makes the decisions, but who decides what decisions are to be made in the first place. In other words, who gets to decide what gets decided. It was Peter Bachrach and Morton S. Baratz (1962) who developed this notion in their influential essay, the *Two Faces of Power*, which differentiated between overt and covert forms. The aim of the second dimension of power is to maintain the status quo, so that those in power stay in power and continue to have their interests served. This theory comes with methodological complications in terms of how to analyze these veiled dynamics, since such activities tend not to take place in open public life.

Steven Lukes took this further, and argued that there was another type of power that was even more hidden than the covert power theorized by Bachrach and Baratz, and therefore even more effective. He suggested that there was an insidious third dimension of power (1974), one that involved people having their beliefs and preferences shaped and affected by the powerful, often without them even realizing. A good example to illustrate this is the work of Edward Bernays, the nephew of Sigmund Freud and founding father of public relations. Bernays rapidly increased the sales of *Lucky Strike* cigarettes by tackling the social taboo of women smoking in public. He drew inspiration from the techniques of psychoanalysis to connect the taboo around smoking with the suffrage movement. Bernays took advantage of the annual Easter parade in New York City in 1929 and asked rich debutantes to take part in a public march and to hide cigarettes on their person. At the same time, he simultaneously tipped off the press, incorrectly informing them that the suffragettes were planning to smoke in public as a protest. At a given moment, the young women had been instructed by Bernays to raise aloft their cigarettes, declaring them "torches of freedom." This spectacle was instantly captured by the cameras and immortalized in print, in turn glamourizing smoking, driving up sales of Lucky Strikes, and abolishing the social taboo.

Lukes argued that it is this form of power that is the most powerful of all. It is the most effective because it is the power to influence the beliefs and ideas of others, inducing them to desire things, even if these things are in opposition to what would benefit them or be in their interests. So ordinary people, or those who are powerless, can show apparent consensus in their own manipulation in order to serve the powerful. According to Lukes, this idea of framing someone else's choices does not even have to happen deliberately or with intent. He asserted that this third dimension of power is the most effective because it is the least observable. It is difficult to subject it to scrutiny and analysis, making it all the more pernicious. There is an obvious point of connection here with Pierre Bourdieu's notion of "symbolic violence," explained by the sociologist as: "the violence which is exercised upon a social agent with his or her complicity" (Bourdieu and Wacquant 2002:167). So this is the kind of domination, both apparent as well as unconscious, that people propagate in everyday life. Due to the normalization of these actions and the way that they are practiced and repeated within so-called legitimate institutions and situations (for example, in the home, school or the workplace, as well as through adverts, films, and other cultural means), they are often unnoticed and reaffirmed.

This idea of the power to shape desires and beliefs maps very neatly onto the concept of soft power. In the words of Joseph Nye (2004:2), soft power is the ability "to influence the behavior of others to get the outcomes one wants." Soft power can therefore reside both in the realm of the imagination, as well as within some kind of operationalized action. Soft power involves the assimilation of thoughts, beliefs and values, through sometimes subtle and imperceptible means. If this is Nye's understanding of soft power, then it is Lukes's third dimension of power that is brought to mind.

The global political stage adds another layer of complexity to this. Nye tells us that power is like the weather and like love, but it is unclear what he means. Does it mean that it is omnipresent? Is he suggesting that we are preoccupied by it? Does it mean that we are at the mercy of it? Does Nye believe that we can use our personal charm to make someone fall in love with us, as we might attract and seduce a lover? Sovereign states are not individuals. They have no higher authority to answer to and they usually act in their own self-interests. They can do what they like, within the accepted boundaries of international norms, rules and principles, and even then, there are frequent transgressions. Sometimes the motives of states are transparent and their movements and actions predictable, but often they are acting in an environment of instability or even anarchy, some might argue. One state does not simply have power over another, instead power is "chaotically distributed" (Nye in

Parmar and Cox 2010:7). Power is also diffused. International relations theorists remind us that the international system involves a range of state and non-state actors, such as intergovernmental and non-governmental organizations, multinational corporations, the media, cultural institutions, and so on. In the words of Joseph Nye, "world politics today is like a three-dimensional chess game" (2010:7), incorporating military power, and economic and transnational relations. There are various schools of thought within international relations that involve different theoretical standpoints to consider the role of the state, whether states act in their own self-interest, what responsibility they have to the international community, how they interact with each other on a global level, how their ideological and moral commitments shape their policies and actions, and how they understand and relate to power. It could also be reasonably argued that all three dimensions of power are simultaneously at play and are often in (literal and metaphorical) conflict with one another.

There are a wide variety of examples to illustrate this complexity. One current case is the ambivalent relationship between Russia and the West. Russia used its power within the United Nations Security Council to veto economic sanctions and military intervention against President Bashar al-Assad, despite it being widely known that the Syrian leader has used chemical weapons on his own people. Russia has a longstanding history of selling arms to the Syrian government and recently joined in the military action against the rebel forces challenging the president, of which there are over 1,000 opposition groups (British Broadcasting Corporation 2013). On the other side is Britain, the United States, and a range of European countries, which are seeking to remove President Assad from power due to his brutal regime against Syrian civilians. Russia does not want to lose its foothold in the Middle East and wants to be seen as a global player (and equal to the United States), and on top of this, seeks to resist Western (particularly American) expansionism. To add to this, these opposing parties are united against a common enemy: the barbaric Islamic State terrorists. At the same time, countries in the European Union and the United States have imposed economic sanctions on Russia for its military intervention in the Ukraine and the annexation of Crimea. These restrictions have contributed to the country's recent financial turmoil with the fall in oil prices and the collapse of the ruble. While this is just one briefly sketched example, it tells us that politics is not a zero-sum game. Rather, it says something about the complexities, contradictions, contestations, and agonisms of world politics today.

[...]

CHAPTER 2

Is Diplomacy an Effective Way to Engage with Hostile States?

Soft Power Is One of Many Ways to Counter Hostile States

Robert McMahon

Robert McMahon is a journalist and the managing editor of the Council on Foreign Relations' website.

Deciding whether or how to engage with the leaders of hostile states has been a matter of debate among US policymakers for decades. In the post-9/11 world, it has become increasingly controversial as national security officials weigh the merits of negotiating with states seen as pursuing weapons of mass destruction as well as non-state actors posing a threat to US targets or US allies. This debate rages continually in the foreign policy community, and during presidential election years like 2008, it has often burst into the open.

Containment and Contacts

Presidents have historically maintained diplomatic—and summit-level—contacts with adversarial states, although the timing and purpose of such engagement has sometimes met criticism. The most often-cited example is the Soviet Union. The United States was committed to maintaining dialogue with the Soviet Union from the early days of the Cold War while seeking to check Soviet influence and expansion—the underpinning of the containment policy accepted by top foreign policy officials of both major political parties. But containment and the notion of maintaining high-level contacts with the Soviets, such as President Dwight D. Eisenhower's 1959 invitation to Soviet leader Nikita Khrushchev to visit the United States, generated resentment from some US conservatives. Conservative commentator William F. Buckley, Jr., told a rally at Carnegie Hall in 1960 that Eisenhower's "diplomatic

"Negotiating with Hostile States," by Robert McMahon, Council on Foreign Relations, June 2, 2008. Reprinted by permission.

sentimentality … can only confirm Khrushchev in the contempt he feels for the dissipated morale of a nation far gone, as the theorists of Marxism have all along contended, in decrepitude."

Critics of engagement also seized on President John F. Kennedy's meeting with Khrushchev in June 1961, five months after his inauguration, as an example of a poorly prepared summit. Some experts say the meeting gave the Soviet leader a chance to lecture the young president at length. Writing in a May 2008 *New York Times* op-ed, Nathan Thrall and Jesse James Wilkins suggest Khrushchev emerged from the encounter emboldened; he followed up by green-lighting the Berlin Wall and shipping nuclear missiles to Cuba. At the same time, historians say Kennedy's deft handling of negotiations with the Soviets during the autumn 1962 Cuban Missile Crisis averted a major confrontation. Within a year, the two nations established a "hotline" to improve communications and signed the Limited Test Ban Treaty, the first international agreement on nuclear weapons.

The Détente Experiment

Republican President Richard M. Nixon accelerated contacts with Soviet leaders in the early 1970s. Nixon and his national security adviser, Henry Kissinger, introduced a policy of détente that aimed to establish new linkages on issues ranging from arms control to improved trade terms. The goal was to lessen superpower tensions as well as induce positive changes in Soviet international behavior. Kissinger writes in his book *Diplomacy* that Nixon's advisers "saw no contradiction in treating the communist world as both adversary and collaborator: adversary in fundamental ideology and in the need to prevent communism from upsetting the global equilibrium; collaborator in keeping the ideological conflict from exploding into a nuclear war."

The new contacts bore fruit in the signing of the Strategic Arms Limitation Treaty (SALT I) in 1972 by Nixon and Soviet leader Leonid Brezhnev. But within a year, tensions related to the October 1973 Arab-Israeli War showed superpower competition remained vigorous, at one point prompting a heightened nuclear alert for US forces. In 1974, congressional critics of détente, led by Democratic Sen. Henry M. Jackson, sidelined a US-Soviet trade agreement with the Jackson-Vanik amendment, which linked trade to emigration of Soviet Jews. Writing in *Foreign Affairs*, historian John Lewis Gaddis called détente a "sophisticated and far-sighted strategy" that Nixon and Kissinger failed to put across to their "own bureaucracies, the Congress, or the public as a whole." Robert S. Litwak, director of international security studies at the Woodrow Wilson Center, writes in his book *Rogue States and U.S. Foreign Policy* that the détente policy was hampered by the "Soviet leadership's ability to compartmentalize relations and frustrate the Nixon administration's efforts to establish linkages."

Some Cold War analysts say more effective as a counterweight to Soviet ambitions was the Nixon administration's simultaneous diplomacy with China, which led to the formal establishment of a dialogue with the 1972 Shanghai Communique. While not posing the direct threat that the Soviet Union represented, Communist China was viewed as no less odious by critics of the Nixon negotiations due to its intervention on North Korea's side in the Korean War, and because of massive human rights abuses, especially in the 1966–1976 Cultural Revolution. Despite such concerns, Nixon saw value in ending China's isolation. He wrote in an October 1967 *Foreign Affairs* article: "We simply cannot afford to leave China forever outside the family of nations, there to nurture its fantasies, cherish its hates and threaten its neighbors."

In the years that followed, US administrations held a number of adversarial states at arm's length, diplomatically. These states included Fidel Castro's Cuba, Vietnam, North Korea, Libya, Nicaragua, Syria, and Sudan. In some cases, like Vietnam, diplomatic ties have been fully restored. In others, such as North Korea, dialogue has resumed over the issue of the country's denuclearization. Relations with Iran were severed after the 1979 seizure of the US embassy, and diplomatic contacts have occurred only sporadically since then. High-level contacts with

Cuba remained a remote prospect in 2008 as an economic embargo continued over US concern at political repression.

President Ronald Reagan took office signaling a tough posture toward the Soviet Union and an intention to stanch communist support for rebellions in Central America. But Reagan also stepped up negotiations on nuclear arms control and participated in summits with Soviet leader Mikhail Gorbachev, a practice continued by George H.W. Bush until the Soviet Union's collapse. In the 1990s, the Clinton administration pursued dialogue with Pyongyang and normalized relations with Vietnam, while seeking to contain and isolate Saddam Hussein's regime in Iraq, and Afghanistan's Taliban leadership.

Engagement with Iran

The issue of speaking to "rogue states" arose in the 2008 presidential campaign after Sen. Barack Obama (D-IL) said in July 2007 that he would meet unconditionally with the leaders of states like Iran, Syria, and Cuba in his first year in office. He dismissed the Bush administration policy of withholding high-level talks as "ridiculous." Obama drew criticism from main Democratic rival Sen. Hillary Clinton (D-NY) and later from Republican candidate Sen. John McCain (R-AZ), both of whom said his willingness for such talks betrayed a naiveté about summit-level discussions with adversaries. The debate, which intensified in mid-2008, has also drawn attention to the Bush administration's mixed record of engaging and isolating states deemed as rogues.

Iran, under international pressure to cease its uranium-enrichment program, represents an especially vexing case for US policymakers. The Bush administration has conditioned broader talks with Iran on the country's agreement to suspend its uranium-enrichment program, which Washington and a number of Western states believe is cover for a nuclear-weapons program. Iran denies this and has refused to suspend its nuclear program. Secretary of State Condoleezza Rice said in repeated interviews in May 2008 that the United States has created an ample framework for a full range of discussions with Iran: "The question isn't why we won't talk to Tehran," she said. "The question is why won't Tehran talk to us?"

As CFR President Emeritus Leslie H. Gelb wrote in an April 2008 op-ed: "The real issue is not whether to talk to the bad guys but how—under which conditions, with which mix of pressure and conciliation, and with what degree of expectation that the bad guys will keep their word." A 2004 CFR Independent Task Force report on Iran called for selective engagement but also advised the executive branch to lay out the framework for formal dialogue with Tehran, along the lines of the Shanghai Communique.

But President Bush has raised doubts about dealings with Iranian President Mahmoud Ahmadinejad, pointing to his militantly anti-Israeli rhetoric. In a widely cited May 15 speech to the Israeli parliament, Bush cited the rhetoric of Ahmadinejad as well as leaders of Hamas and Hezbollah and made references to the appeasement of Nazi Germany in the 1930s. "Some seem to believe that we should negotiate with the terrorists and radicals, as if some ingenious argument will persuade them they have been wrong all along," Bush said. "We have an obligation to call this what it is—the false comfort of appeasement, which has been repeatedly discredited by history."

Terrorism expert Bruce Hoffman, a professor at Georgetown's School of Foreign Service, says Iran poses a challenge because of its multiple poles of power. However, he believes Washington should be committed to negotiations to try to work out its differences with the regime. "We negotiated with the Iranians when they were holding fifty-two diplomats hostage [in 1979]," Hoffman said. "I don't see it as a sign of weakness to say we are going to negotiate on issues even more consequential."

Some regional analysts say Iran's odd political identity makes dealing with its current leadership tricky. Iranian-born author Amin Taheri writes in a May 2008 *Wall Street Journal* op-ed that Iran is still passing through an identity crisis of sorts: "The Islamic Republic does not know how to behave: as a nation-state, or as the embodiment of a revolution with universal messianic pretensions. Is it a country or a cause?" Michael Rubin of the American Enterprise Institute writes in a May 2007 CFR.org Online Debate that dealing with Iran's elected leaders could be fruitless. "If engagement is to be successful, it must include the sincere involvement of the people who control those aspects of regime behavior which Washington finds most objectionable—this means the Supreme Leader and the Revolutionary Guards. This is an unlikely prospect," he writes.

Presidential candidates Obama and Clinton have faulted the Bush administration for failing to exert more energy on diplomacy with Iran. Obama has gone a step further by indicating he would be interested in meeting with Iranian leaders without making meetings contingent on suspension of uranium enrichment, although he subsequently indicated that some lower-level preparatory talks would be necessary. McCain, the presumptive Republican nominee, has spoken out against meeting the Iranian president. He has indicated he would continue the Bush administration's approach of offering inducements to Iran if it suspends enrichment while stepping up efforts to isolate the regime if it fails to cooperate, including a global divestment campaign.

The 9/11 Effect

National security experts note the US strategy for dealing with rogue regimes changed after the 9/11 terrorist attacks on New York and Washington. In a June 2002 speech at West Point, President Bush said: "containment is not possible when unbalanced dictators with weapons of mass destruction can deliver those weapons on missiles or secretly provide them to terrorist allies." The Bush administration's National Security Strategy, issued in September 2002, asserted the need for preemptive strikes against states or entities intent on terrorism. This language "reflected the view that the bad behavior of these regimes was inextricably linked to their character," says the Wilson Center's Litwak. "Hence, a change of conduct or behavior would be inadequate because the behavior derived from the regime's character. Therefore, you had to change the regime to end the behavior."

The preemptive-strike policy was employed in the March 2003 invasion that ousted Iraqi dictator Saddam Hussein, whose regime was accused of developing weapons of mass destruction (WMD) that posed a threat to the United States. But in the case of Libya, which was linked to multiple terrorist attacks and was developing its own WMD programs, the Bush administration tried a different tack that relied more on diplomacy. Washington gained a Libyan agreement to dismantle its WMD programs and renounce terrorism in 2003 in exchange for US assistance in opening economic and political ties.

Debate continues over the usefulness of negotiations with an Iran seen as intent on developing nuclear weapons. John Bolton, a former top arms-control official and UN ambassador in the Bush administration, warned in a May 2008 *Wall Street Journal* op-ed of a reliance on negotiation with states or entities intent on supporting weapons or developing dangerous weapons. "In today's world of weapons of mass destruction, time is again a precious asset, one almost invariably on the side of the would-be proliferators," Bolton wrote. "Time allows them to perfect the complex science and technology necessary to sustain nuclear weapons and missile programs, and provides far greater opportunity for concealing their activities from our ability to detect and, if necessary, destroy them."

Stateless Rogues

The US refusal to recognize or negotiate with non-state terror groups predated 9/11, although there have been nuances in US policy before and after the attacks, as this Backgrounder notes. Experts from both major US political parties appear to be united on opposing diplomatic talks with stateless parties linked to terrorism such as Hamas and Hezbollah. Obama, Clinton, and McCain have all said they would not hold talks with the leaders of either group. The Bush administration refuses contacts as well, although a top

US diplomat called the May 21, 2008, power-sharing deal that gave Hezbollah a blocking majority in the Lebanese cabinet a "necessary and positive step."

Former diplomat Dennis Ross believes negotiations can be used to alter the behavior of other states, but in a May 2008 op-ed he wrote that non-state actors like Hamas and Hezbollah must meet a higher threshold before talks are justified. "If achieving legitimacy is so important to them—if proving that they don't need to adjust to the world, but proving that the world must adjust to them is such a central aim of theirs—then it is essential that they not get something for nothing," Ross wrote. "They should be required to meet certain conditions before we negotiate with them." Terrorism expert Hoffman adds that a goal of counterterrorism strategy "should always be to isolate the violent extremists and to try to prevent otherwise nonviolent extremists from becoming violent." Some weakening of terrorist groups should occur before negotiations start, he says, so that states are not "negotiating out of fear."

A Mixed Record

A number of experts on diplomacy and terrorism point to mixed messages from the Bush administration on dealing with rogue states. It has named an envoy for Sudan to deal with a Sudanese leadership the administration accuses of genocide. It has engaged North Korea in denuclearization talks after initially labeling it in 2002 part of an "axis of evil," and it has continued those talks even amid recent signals Pyongyang was providing nuclear technology to Syria. Talks continue with Iran, through European interlocutors. "We are caught between precedents," says the Wilson Center's Litwak. "We can't replicate the Iraq model and it's not been clear that we're prepared to offer the Libya model," which included removing the threat of regime change.

Soft Power Can Transform How Countries See One Another

Mark Leonard

Mark Leonard is the cofounder and director of the European Council on Foreign Relations.

During the Cold War, the United States created a robust array of cultural and intellectual instruments to spread American values behind the Iron Curtain and plead the US case to nonaligned nations. After the fall of the Berlin Wall, the United States gradually dismantled many of these propaganda and information tools, emasculating the United States Information Agency and paring the Voice of America and Radio Free Europe down to almost residual proportions. Other countries followed suit, such as when the British initially slashed the budget of the BBC World Service and the Germans scaled back their efforts at cultural promotion by closing down branches of their Goethe-Instituts all over the world.

Ironically, the end of the Cold War has made public diplomacy—the task of communicating with overseas publics—more important than ever. The spread of democracy to a majority of countries, increased access to news and information, and the rise of global nongovernmental organizations (NGOs) and protest movements have put ever greater constraints on national governments. The disparate public reaction to the attacks of September 11, 2001, and their aftermath has made that point all too clear. As Western governments strive to convince reluctant allies in the Muslim world that the war against terrorism is not a war against Islam, the "battle for hearts and minds" has risen once again to the top of policymakers' in boxes.

"Diplomacy by Other Means," by Mark Leonard, *Foreign Policy*, November 9, 2009. Reprinted by permission.

The last decade is rife with examples of popular perceptions, rather than governments, setting the pace for international diplomacy. In Kosovo, a powerful military coalition risked defeat not in the field but in the media battleground for public support as governments in Greece and Italy struggled to cope with volatile popular opinion. In Rwanda, ethnic conflict was mobilized through inflammatory radio broadcasts to civilians rather than by military command chains. Recent anti-globalization demonstrations have revealed a new diplomatic environment where state and nonstate actors compete for the public's attention. After the mad cow disease crisis in Britain, the French government violated European Union law and continued to ban British beef, largely in response to public fears about safety. And the global competition for investment, trade, tourists, entrepreneurs, and highly skilled workers extends the influence of foreign publics beyond the political to the economic.

The common thread throughout these disparate examples is public perception: The way in which foreign publics interpret British, US, or other countries' values, motivations, and qualities can create an enabling or a disabling environment. Propaganda will not persuade populations in reluctant countries to support war, but perceptions of Western motivations as imperial or self-interested can damage the chances of success. The BBC will not block out calls to arms from tribal radio stations, but it can act as a counterweight if people trust its dispassionate overview of ethnic tensions. Promotional advertisements for British beef might have a limited impact on consumers' fears, but efforts to show the quality of British science and the integrity of its veterinarians could help mollify French suspicions. And campaigns to change the perceptions of countries like Ireland, Spain, and New Zealand created a premium for products and services and helped attract investment and tourists.

All transactions and points of contact—whether promoting policies, selling products, or attracting investment—will feed off the general image of a country and reflect back onto it, in both positive and negative directions. For example, Norway's reputation for work in international mediation will help persuade the different factions in Sri Lanka that Norway is an honest broker, which will in turn add to Norway's reputation for peace. Equally, when the United States tries to exempt its peacekeepers from prosecution by the International Criminal Court, such action reinforces the US reputation for double standards and unilateralism.

Joseph S. Nye Jr., dean of the John F. Kennedy School of Government at Harvard University, has argued that the power of influence can complement more traditional forms of power based on economic or military clout. Such "soft power," he notes, can rest on the appeal of "one's ideas or the ability to set the agenda in ways that shape the preferences of others." But governments have yet to remold their own diplomatic structures to adapt to this changed environment. Instead, most diplomatic institutions have done little more than bolt on a few new units or recruit a couple of extra staff from NGOs—changes that are essentially cosmetic. Instead, diplomats must transform themselves from reporters and lobbyists who react to issues into shapers of public debates around the world.

To Sell the Truth

The term "public diplomacy" is often a euphemism for propaganda. But the proliferation of information in open societies (and, increasingly, in closed ones as well) makes it more difficult for governments to control information. Attempts to distort the truth will eventually be exposed and therefore will create even greater skepticism of governments. Moreover, because most ideas that people absorb about a country are beyond the control of national governments—books, cds, films, television programs, or brands and consumer products with national connotations—governments can only have an impact at the margins by seeking to clear paths for the most positive messages to reach mass audiences while working directly to influence the opinions of niche audiences.

Public diplomacy should be about building relationships, starting from understanding other countries' needs, cultures, and peoples and then looking for areas to make common cause. As the relationships deepen, public diplomacy can achieve a hierarchy of objectives: increasing familiarity (making people think about your country and updating their images of it); increasing appreciation (creating positive perceptions of your country and getting others to see issues from your perspective); engaging people (encouraging people to see your country as an attractive destination for tourism and study and encouraging them to buy its products and subscribe to its values); and influencing people's behavior (getting companies to invest, encouraging public support for your country's positions, and convincing politicians to turn to it as an ally).

To achieve these goals, governments must craft a public diplomacy that operates in three dimensions. The first is communication on day-to-day issues—in other words, aligning traditional diplomacy with the news cycle. The globalization of news coverage complicates this task. Diplomats have no control over the way the media present their countries, since those reports are typically filed by foreign correspondents. Some of the stories that have the biggest impact abroad are not traditional foreign policy stories that embassies are equipped to deal with but are domestic stories, such as the outbreak of foot-and-mouth disease in Britain, the success of right-wing politician Jean-Marie Le Pen in the recent French presidential elections, or the desecration of Jewish graves in Italy. Diplomats will talk to the press about "foreign" news stories, but they will refer enquiries about "domestic" stories to the relevant government departments, which are not equipped to understand the international repercussions of their actions. Moreover, during the throes of a domestic crisis, foreign correspondents will invariably get second-class service since government officials will be primarily concerned about press coverage at home.

The second dimension of public diplomacy is strategic communication. Governments are adept at conveying their stances on particular issues (whether tariffs on steel or peacemaking in the Middle East), but officials are much less effective at managing overall perceptions of their country. One reason for this failure is that different institutions have been responsible for dealing with politics, trade, tourism, investment, and cultural relations. But on many issues, the totality of messages will determine how people abroad relate to a nation.

Strategic communication is like a political campaign: developing a set of comprehensive messages and planning a series of symbolic events and photo opportunities to reinforce them. Chris Powell, chairman of the British advertising company BMP DDB, argues that since people are exposed to thousands of messages every day, the themes must not be overly complex: "A contrast between diplomacy and advertising is that in advertising an enormous amount of work goes into the preparation—boiling ideas down into very, very simple concepts, and then repeating that message over and over again until we are all thoroughly bored with it. When you are so bored with it that you feel like giving up, the listener may just have begun to register the message."

The third dimension of public diplomacy is the most long term: developing lasting relationships with key individuals through scholarships, exchanges, training, seminars, conferences, and access to media channels. This approach differs from the usual diplomatic practice of nurturing contacts through lunches, cocktail parties, and receptions. These relationships are not built between diplomats and people abroad—they are between peers (politicians, special advisors, business people, cultural entrepreneurs, and academics). This approach differs from messages designed to sell because it involves a genuine exchange that leads to a "warts and all" picture of the country.

Hearing It Like It Is

Many of the communication initiatives that Western governments developed after the terrorist attacks last autumn fall into what can best be described as a "conveyor belt" model for transmitting information. Recent debates about public diplomacy—particularly in the United States, but in other countries as well—suggest that many policymakers feel the key problem is a lack of information, as if to say, "If only other people had access to the same degree of information we have, and the same degree of insight, then they would agree with us."

But post-September 11 public diplomacy has not failed to deliver information. Rather, it has failed to deliver information convincingly. The tone of many messages is declamatory, without any apparent intent to engage in dialogue or listen. For instance, immediately after September 11, 2001, the US government resorted to crude psychological operations such as dropping leaflet bombs (showing a member of the Taliban beating a group of women and bearing the message: "Is this the future you want for your children and your women?") or dropping fixed-frequency windup radios tuned to US military broadcasts.

If Western governments are to move beyond propaganda, they must meet four challenges: understanding the target audience, confronting hostility toward Western culture, engaging people emotionally, and proving their own relevance to the public concerned.

Knowing your audience is the top priority for any effective communication. But diplomats are often more interested in winning arguments than in persuading skeptical publics. Governments struggle to internalize and prepare for potential threats that do not conform to their underlying strategic assumptions. This mind-set explains why the Iranian revolution in 1979 was such a massive shock to Western diplomats. The signs were there—rising social unrest, the growing influence of Islamic political activists—but the bureaucratic mandarins couldn't accept them.

Carrying out successful diplomacy is difficult if you do not have ears for things you do not want to hear. Both the British Foreign and Commonwealth Office and the US State Department fell into this trap when they produced leaflets about the attacks on the World Trade Center and the Pentagon. Although the leaflets contained shocking pictures that worked on an emotional level, the text was very forensic, explaining why the September 11 attacks were undoubtedly carried out by Osama bin Laden. These sorts of messages become enmeshed in a battleground of "your information versus my information."

As the former advertising executives Adam Lury (of HHCL and Partners) and Simon Gibson (of Saatchi & Saatchi) put it: "The answer is not more information, but a different form of engagement." That sentiment led US Under Secretary of State for Public Diplomacy and Public Affairs Charlotte Beers to advise US public affairs officers, "Our goal is not what you say, but the response that you desire." Public diplomacy is not simply delivering a message to an audience; it is about getting a result. And to get a result, you need to acknowledge that the listener's views matter as much as the message. You must therefore be ready to explore the legitimacy of some basic beliefs—from human and gender rights to health and safety—in different societies and to discuss how they will work in practice, rather than repeating them by rote.

The second step toward effective communication involves countering the widespread anger at what is perceived to be a one-way flow of culture from the West. The belief that local customs, histories, and identities are being swallowed by the unstoppable advance of Gap, Starbucks, and Tom Cruise presents diplomats with an inherently hostile audience.

The right message and positioning on a topic can prevent weak arguments from falling on deaf ears. Consider, for example, the recent repositioning of French public diplomacy, which used to be based on pushing French cultural exceptionalism and promoting the French language. With the creation of a new public diplomacy department, the French developed a novel approach: Instead of promoting French exceptionalism, the French government sought common cause with other countries on the receiving end of US cultural dominance and positioned themselves as the champion of those nations. In a similar maneuver, when it became apparent that French could not compete with English as a global language, France sought to promote multi-lingualism; if French will not be the first foreign language learned around the world, then at least more than one foreign language will be learned.

Western governments would do well to emphasize pluralism as a central part of their identities and to illustrate the impact that foreign cultures have on their countries. One successful example is a British program called Visiting Arts. By bringing artists and performers from other cultures to the United Kingdom, the government presents a very positive image of a receptive British culture, which plays well in the proud originating country and helps to dispel concerns about cultural hegemony or British domination of the developing world. Contrast this approach with that of the US State Department, which plans to air short videos on Arab television channels profiling the lives of "ordinary" Muslim-Americans, including teachers, basketball players, and firefighters. The intended message is that the United States is an open society, tolerant and accepting of all religions, but the videos might prove counterproductive since they portray Muslims as being assimilated into US culture.

The third challenge to public diplomacy is to move beyond intellectual forms of communication. Recent advertisements for the Morgan Stanley Dean Witter credit card assert that 93 percent of all communication is nonverbal. It is difficult to trust that exact figure, but it is clear that many other factors—experiences, emotions, images—influence people's responses to messages. The challenge is to move from supplying information to capturing the imagination.

The British ambassador to the United States, Sir Christopher Meyer, explained the importance of symbolism in Washington, D.C., after September 11: "The British stock has never been higher in the US. It is a combination of words and symbols ... First, [Prime Minister Tony] Blair saying 'it is an attack on us all.' Then on September 13th the playing of the Star-Spangled Banner at the changing of the guard at Buckingham Palace. And third, when the president made his address to Congress, there was Blair up in the gallery showing his support. The combination of these events produced a surge of affection for the U.K. What we are really saying to Americans is that we are the only people in the entire cosmos whom you can really count on when the going gets tough."

The fourth challenge to transcending propagandist messages is proving your relevance. While that might not typically be a problem for the United States, other countries often fall short. One way of demonstrating relevance is to concentrate on "niche diplomacy." Norway is a good example of a country that has a voice and a presence on the international stage out of proportion to its modest position and assets. It has achieved this presence through a ruthless prioritization of its target audiences and its concentration on a single message: Norway as a force for peace. This reputation gives Norway greater visibility than its size warrants and rebuts accusations of isolationism. Main activities in this field include Norway's large foreign-aid budget (second-most among industrialized countries as a percentage of gross national product) and its conflict resolution efforts in the Middle East (the Oslo accords), Sri Lanka, and Colombia. Norway also operates a rapid-reaction force (the Norwegian Resource Bank for Democracy and Human Rights) to assist in election monitoring and conflict prevention in about 20 countries annually. The Nobel Peace Prize, originating in Oslo, is a happy historical fact that also raises Norway's profile.

Shoot the Messenger

Effective public diplomacy relies on more than just the quality of a message. Sometimes, the problem is the messenger. Even the most well-crafted argument will fall flat if nobody trusts the source. Just as readers might be skeptical of an article appearing in a newspaper with an extreme ideological slant, so too might a target audience be leery of an information campaign sponsored by a Western government with a perceived political motive.

The traditional approach to public diplomacy activity overseas, be it cultural festivals, seminars, economic promotion, or policy advocacy, is that it should all be concluded with "a few words from the ambassador." In some cases, it would be far more useful to keep the ambassador indoors. Sensitive messages to foreign publics are often best disseminated by people who have something in common with the target audience. For instance, the decision to arrange visits of prominent Muslims living in Britain to Islamic countries after September 11 more convincingly demonstrated British respect for Islam than did any ministerial pronouncements.

If a message will engender distrust simply because it is coming from a foreign government, then the government should hide that fact as much as possible. Increasingly, if a state is to make its voice heard and to influence events outside its direct control, it must work through organizations and networks that are separate from, independent of, and even suspicious of governments themselves. Three of the most effective mediums for this type of public diplomacy are NGOs, diasporas, and political parties.

Nongovernmental Organizations

Working with nonstate actors, such as NGOs, is central to communication with civil societies in other countries (and hence central to influencing their governments) because NGOs have three key resources not readily available to foreign governments:

credibility, expertise, and appropriate networks. People are often quick to question the motivations behind the diplomatic pronouncements of a state, but NGOs such as Human Rights Watch or Oxfam have a long-standing reputation for independence—and hence a credibility—that it is not feasible for a government to create for itself. (Amnesty International's recent condemnation of Palestinian suicide bombings, for instance, had a much more profound impact on political discourse than countless denunciations from the US and Israeli governments.) The Canadian polling company Environics International surveyed 1,000 people in each of the Group of 20 industrialized and developing countries and found that 65 percent of people trust NGOs to work in the best interests of society, while only 45 percent trust national governments to do the same.

NGOs have access to networks of activists, experts, and foreign politicians—and they know how to marshal those networks to exert pressure in a given policy area. No diplomatic mission possesses (or would wish to possess) the capability to organize street demonstrations, nor are diplomats well positioned to coordinate sustained lobbying campaigns. More than 20,000 transnational NGO networks are already active on the world stage (of which 90 percent were created during the last 30 years), and many of them could make effective partners for conducting public diplomacy. Governments, however, should be clear-eyed about such relationships, because they bring their own peculiar difficulties. NGOs have a much more informal way of doing things and tend to work on a "want-to-know," rather than a "need-to-know," basis.

Despite this clash of cultures, collaborations between NGOs and governments have yielded several notable successes. For example, efforts to restrict the global trade in smuggled "conflict diamonds"—which funded some of Africa's bloodiest civil wars in Sierra Leone, Angola, and the Democratic Republic of the Congo—would not have been successful without sustained government action alongside NGOs like Global Witness and Human Rights

Watch and representatives from the diamond industry, particularly De Beers and the World Diamond Council.

Diasporas

Thanks to increased international migration during the latter half of the 20th century, there are now "living links"—relations, friends, former business partners—within virtually every country in the world. The untapped potential in the global diaspora could, with sustained involvement, yield several advantages to policymakers. First, and most obviously, diasporas can help fill the demand for language skills that has been highlighted by the events following September 11, when Pashto, Farsi, and Arabic speakers were much needed.

Furthermore, such links provide the cultural knowledge, political insight, and human intelligence necessary for a successful foreign policy. The mistakes and disasters that marked events like the Vietnam War or the Iranian Revolution, for instance, might have been avoided had there been more comprehensive and intimate knowledge of those societies available to policymakers. Daniel Ellsberg, the defense analyst who leaked the Pentagon Papers on US decision making in Vietnam, has said that no high-ranking US official at the time of the war's escalation "could have passed in office a midterm freshman exam in modern Vietnamese history ..."

An important and easily overlooked aspect of diaspora diplomacy is the complexity of relations between different expatriates of the same country. A recent focus group the Foreign Policy Centre conducted with young professionals in New Delhi revealed very different attitudes toward the Indian diaspora in the United States and the United Kingdom. Many thought of their compatriots in the United Kingdom as low-skilled, low-wage, and unmotivated—an image essentially dominated by the corner shop and the import-export trade. In stark contrast, the US Indian community was seen in a more positive light, as ambitious and highly skilled—an image heavily influenced by the perceived prevalence of Indians in the information-technology industry of Silicon Valley. Governments, therefore, should not just pay attention to improving the image of their countries but also to the image of resident diaspora communities.

Political Parties

A third area where non-government-to-government diplomacy could be very fruitful is in building relations between political parties in different countries. Problems between governments may appear to be diplomatic when, in fact, they stem from difficulties that revolve around perceived political differences. For example, one important contributing factor to the frosty relations that have sometimes prevailed between Britain and France during the last few years has been the suspicion among some members of the French left toward New Labour's perceived neoliberal tilt.

The relations between political parties of the same broad stripe in different countries can be a vitally important dimension of those nations' overall foreign relations. On a growing list of issues—economic reform, social rights, agriculture, drugs, terrorism, and the environment, not to mention humanitarian intervention—national interests are neither immutable nor particular to a single country. Instead, such issues can only be addressed through a deliberative political process. Increased links between political parties represent one way to deal with that historic shift.

Some countries are already fostering such relations. One example is Germany's Konrad Adenauer Stiftung—a large, politically oriented institute affiliated with the Christian Democratic movement, which receives substantial state funding to facilitate policy debate and exchanges between countries and to maintain a physical presence in dozens of nations. German taxpayers fund similar organizations with links to the other main parties: the Social Democrats, Liberals, and Greens. This approach has many advantages. First, nurturing relations between politicians of different countries makes diplomacy easier by giving both sides a clear idea of the political positioning of the other. Second, such relationships open a channel for policy exchange that renews the intellectual capital of political parties. Third, exchanges help develop an international outlook within parties that are not in power, which can be advantageous in smoothing the transition between administrations.

No More "Hard Sell"

All governments pay lip service to how the rise of global communications, the spread of democracy, the growth of NGOs, and the development of powerful multilateral organizations have shifted the nature of power within societies and altered the craft of diplomacy. But few have adequately reflected those changes in how they deploy their resources, organize their activities, or go about their core business. It is a paradox that, as interdependence has increased, the effort invested in nurturing relationships with the rest of the world has steadily declined.

The biggest challenge is to the culture and priorities of diplomatic institutions themselves. Public diplomacy can no longer be seen as an add-on to the rest of diplomacy—it must be seen as a central activity that is played out across many dimensions and with many partners. Above all, Western governments need a much broader and more creative idea of what public diplomacy is and what it can do.

Such reforms are already apparent in the United States, as public diplomacy gradually moves away from the browbeating associated with the American "hard sell." The State Department has rebranded the Voice of America's Arabic service as "Radio Sawa" ("Radio Together"). Gone are the hours of US government-monitored talk that attracted a small audience of older decision makers. In its place is a fast-paced music station aimed at the young, who subliminally ingest news bulletins between blasts of Britney Spears and the Backstreet Boys. The United States also plans to launch a 24-hour Arabic satellite news channel that will compete with the mighty Al Jazeera. All these efforts are backed by serious money—a proposed $750 million for promotional materials, cultural and educational exchanges, and radio and television channels in the Middle East.

But a communications strategy can't work if it cuts against the grain of a country's foreign policy. It will be impossible for the United States to win hearts and minds unless the targeted people get a sense that the United States really cares about them as individuals, not just because they are seen as potential terrorists. The current US administration has demonstrated that it values coercion above all else. As such, public diplomacy still will be seen as the projection of power. Unilateralist policies that always put US interests first will undercut sophisticated attempts to build relationships with foreign publics. For all its good intentions, US public diplomacy could become mired by these contradictions—a velvet fist in an iron glove.

Soft Power Creates Stronger Relationships than Hard Power

John Weinbrenner

John Weinbrenner completed his master's degree in political science at the University of Central Florida.

The current state of international relations is often referred to as the unipolar moment due to the uncontested military capabilities and overall prowess of the United States. However, with this power has come resentment and resistance, which ultimately questions how much bona fide influence the most powerful country in the world truly possesses. This paper is an analysis of US power and how it affects influence in the Latin American region. I hypothesize that the traditional use of hard power as the predominant foreign policy method employed towards Latin America has damaged overall US influence. By examining the effects of two historic cases, one that exhibits soft power traits and another that depicts hard power tactics a better understanding of American influence in the region can be attained.

What exactly is the difference between *soft power* and *hard power*? These terms were developed by former Assistant Secretary of Defense and Dean of the Kennedy School of Government at Harvard University Joseph Nye to illustrate the different characteristics of power when used to influence behavior. When power is used to coerce or induce conduct it reflects the concept of hard power. Hard power is typically associated with the realist perspective of international relations theory that mainly asserts power comes from military and economic means. In other words, the ability to financially implement economic sanctions on a nation or unilaterally invade another country with one's army in order to

"Soft Power and Hard Power Approaches in U.S. Foreign Policy: A Case Study Comparison in Latin America," by John Weinbrenner, University of Central Florida, 2007. Used with permission from the author, John M Weinbrenner.

influence the behavior of it are hard power strategies. Therefore, hard power is the ability to *force* the outcomes one wants. Soft power on the other hand refers to the power of *attraction*. Rather than being threatened to a particular outcome actors willingly go along with the preferences of another state, thus "soft power rests on the ability to shape the preferences of others" (Nye, 2004, p.5). Political ideals, popular culture, and cooperation like that found in multilateral organizations can often prompt actors to be attracted to the desires of another country. For example, during the Cold War freedom of political expression along with American pop culture caused many Russians to want what the United States had. At the same time, although soft power attracted the Russian people to the free market system, hard power through America's nuclear arsenal threatened the Soviets from intruding too far into the American sphere of influence. In sum, soft power can be linked to as Nye says, the "co-optive end of the spectrum of behavior, whereas hard-power resources are usually associated with command behavior" (Nye, 2004, p.7).

The specific cases I am utilizing to reflect soft power and hard power tactics will be Franklin Roosevelt's Good Neighbor policy and the contra war in Nicaragua taken place during Ronald Reagan's Administration, respectively. By examining these two dissimilar cases one should be able to uncover which type of power approach leads to more influence in the Latin American region. Influence is vital because it equates to the achievement of American objectives.

The level of American influence in geopolitics has most recently come into question during the current Iraq War. In 2003, the United States led a military coalition in the swift and successful invasion of Iraq. There was little argument that the United States' massive military capacity was the chief reason for the victory, and it is without debate that the United States could have performed equally as triumphant on the battlefield if a "coalition of the willing" had never been formed. However, the current situation of rebuilding war-torn Iraq has proven to be a challenge the United States does not appear to have the power to do alone. In regards to insurgents, radical Islamic fundamentalism, and sectarian violence US influence is absent from the scene. During the early stages, perception of American power was exceedingly high for members of the president's administration and other proponents of the war, thus a genuine attempt to reach out and garner more international support for the invasion did not take place. This has consequentially caused the United States to stand nearly alone in the rebuilding effort while members of the European community toss rebuffs at the country that pulled a deafened ear to their earlier concerns over the war.

While a majority of the world is trying to come to grips with the notion that the United States is the world's sole superpower with considerable unchecked military power, Latin America has had to face such a fact for most of its post-colonial history. For instance, Thomas Jefferson believed it was possible for the United States to take control over Spain's former empire "peice by peice [sic]" (Smith, 2000, p.18). And the interventions that would occur from Teddy Roosevelt's era through the Clinton Administration provided a constant scare that the colossal neighbor to the north had the ability to interject into Latin American affairs at its will. The fact that Latin America was the first to contend with America's undiluted power permits the region to be an interesting study population for an analysis on American power approaches. At the same time it provides reasoning behind why countless scholars claim there to be a troubled relationship between the United States and Latin America.

While a great deal of authors criticize the United States for past policies that they argue have hampered its relationship with Latin America, others contend traditional US policy is the only remedy to fix this troubled relationship and rebuild American influence in the region. For this first camp, their argument often centers on the notion that US policymakers do not fully understand Latin American affairs. As James Reston a foreign correspondent for *The New York Times* once stated, "the United States will do anything [aid, investment, political pressure, military intervention] for Latin

America except read about it" (Wiarda, 2006, p.85). This lack of willingness to learn and have a handle on the affairs of its southern neighbors has consequentially caused difficulties to arise.

Julia Sweig of the Council on Foreign Relations notes that the United States often gathers intelligence about Latin American countries from its elite and powerful citizens rather than from those without power in the general population. She has coined this phenomenon the 80/20 Divide, where American policymakers concern themselves with the interests of the elite sector of a Latin American country while not paying any attention to the remaining eighty percent of the citizenry (Sweig, 2006, p.37). The electoral victory of Hugo Chávez in Venezuela is a prime example of the 80/20 Divide at work. For the past fifty years Sweig notes the United States has gained information about the country from the top twenty percent of Venezuela's private sector, politics, and the oil industry; thus when Chávez came into prominence representing the needs of the unheard majority American policymakers were ignorant to his potential power. Therefore, Sweig asks without an understanding of the desires of the Venezuelan people how was the United States expected to build any influence?

In general it has been argued if it is not a matter of mis-understanding Latin American affairs it is forgetting the effects of past US action that have hurt American influence in the region. In fact, there is an axiom in the history between the United States and Latin America that the United States never remembers and Latin America never forgets. Jorge I. Domínguez wrote in a 2003 article for *Foreign Policy* that "Nicaraguans have much to teach the cabal in Kabul about how the United States forgets its nice rhetoric and apparent commitment to its erstwhile allies" (Domínguez, 2000, p.34). This inability to follow through on promises has often left a feeling of rejection and neglect amongst the Latin American people. Robert Pastor has likened US policy toward the region to a whirlpool because the United States is often sucked into regional crises only to be released as events elsewhere capture American attention (Pastor, 2001, p.ix). This traditional strategy of policy by crisis combined with an array of hard-line unilateral policies from sanctions to military interventions has caused several scholars and former policymakers to make the case for a change in the US stance towards Latin America.

For example, Moisés Naím, the editor in chief of *Foreign Policy* magazine asserts President George W. Bush should make two specific changes, end the embargo with Cuba and actively engage with Brazil. Naím claims US obsession with crises in small nations like Cuba, Grenada, and Haiti have prevented it from focusing on building an influential alliance with Brazil, the largest and arguably most powerful country in Latin America, who could serve as a viable partner in achieving broader US goals (Naím, 2006, p.35).

In addition, former US ambassador Robert White has echoed this cry for less unilateral ventures. White argues the United States should have convoked a meeting with foreign ministers of the Organization of American States (OAS) after the temporary overthrow of democratically elected Chávez in 2002 (White, 2005, p.11). Although Chávez was an obstacle to US goals, the decision to denounce him and praise the illegitimate un-elected regime went against America's values of democracy, for which White contends hurt the US image of representing democratic principles. As a result, US influence diminished as exhibited by the unsuccessful bid of its hand picked candidate for secretary general to the OAS. Member states rejected the American nominee under Chávez's lead, who was now seen as a hero in an event that had "all the elements of a David vs. Goliath morality play" (White, 2005, p.11). White further states, "American failures abroad usually occur when we violate the ideals that undergird our society" (White, 2005, p.11).

This has been the case made by Joseph Nye who claims "those who scorn or despise us for hypocrisy are less likely to want to help us achieve our policy objectives" (Nye, 2004, p.55). In addition to following our own standards, Nye favors the use of cultural exchanges between Americans and citizens of foreign countries to help build lasting relationships, which he argues can ultimately increase US influence. For example, he reports the account of a former high official in the Russian KGB who commented that "exchanges were a Trojan Horse for the Soviet Union" and that "they played a tremendous role in the erosion of the Soviet System" (Nye, 2004, p.46). Nye notes the reduction of funds for public diplomacy, travel bans like that with Cuba, and the overall focus on military hard power as areas where US foreign policy has gone wrong.

However, are Naím, White, and Nye correct to assume a change towards a softer US policy will increase America's influence? In other words, could cultural exchanges with the Venezuelan public not only have prepared the United States for a Chávez electoral victory, but influenced the public to elect another candidate? Moreover, is the traditional hard-line approach truly responsible for less American influence in Latin America today? This thesis is an attempt to answer such questions.

I noted earlier that Latin America offers a valuable study population to analyze US power approaches because of the region's long history of dealing with American ascendancy. Also mentioned above I described my intentions to analyze two notable cases in the history of US Latin American relations, the Good Neighbor policy and the contra war in Nicaragua in order to determine what effect the power approaches used in each of these cases had on immediate and long-term US influence in Latin America. Through this comparative historical case study it should be revealed whether or not soft power tactics like those used during the Good Neighbor policy or hard power techniques such as the ones implemented during the contra war against the Sandinistas produces more influence for the United States in Latin America. Therefore this study should also help explain why several scholars recognize a problem for the United States in its relationship towards the region.

My dependent variable is American influence. This concept refers to the overall sway the United States possesses in Latin America. In general a qualitative approach will be used to determine the variability of influence the United States holds. For instance, judging how easily and successful the accomplishment of subsequent objectives or desires were in the region provides an indicator of how much influence was obtained from that particular power approach. The independent variables soft power and hard power are also codified in a qualitative manner. A detailed explanation on how the Good Neighbor policy and the contra war fit the soft and hard power traits will be addressed in chapter three, nevertheless one should be able to comprehend the difference between soft and hard power using the definitions cited above in the chapter's opening paragraphs. However, the independent variables are certainly not limited to just those indicators, and furthermore it is quite possible after an extensive investigation, although unlikely because they were chosen for their polarity, to claim that my two selected case studies the Good Neighbor policy and the contra war in Nicaragua are a combination of the two power approaches at varying degrees.

The Good Neighbor policy refers to Franklin Roosevelt's foreign policy strategy towards Latin America during his tenure as president. It is a unique moment of time in inter-American relations because of the emphasis put on nonintervention and the importance of public diplomacy, which is a strong characteristic of a soft power approach. The foreign policy techniques used before and after the Good Neighbor era contrast greatly from the events that occurred during Roosevelt's Administration, thus the Good Neighbor policy offers a valuable case for a comparison of power approaches. The contra war in Nicaragua is an equally beneficial case for this study because it reflects hard power policies such as military intervention and economic threats. Furthermore, the extensive use of coercive diplomacy and unilateral action by the Reagan Administration counters elements of the soft power concept. Moreover, as a relatively recent event in hemispheric relations participants in the episode can provide contemporary discussion on the affair's effect on US influence today.

The selection of those two cases I believe best reflects the soft power and hard power approaches and US foreign policy to the region as a whole. Of course, additional events could have also been selected with comparative significance to serve as the independent variables, however due to the constraints of this short study it has been decided to closely examine two events, one related to soft power and the other related to hard power, in greater detail rather than glance at a wide range of very old and perhaps inconsequential events.

I predict my investigation will reveal support for my hypothesis that hard power when not supported by soft power has diminished American influence in Latin America. I have this inclination because there are a number of examples outside of those in my case study that do point to this line of reasoning. As noted above cultural contacts during the Cold War have been cited as a "Trojan Horse" for the Soviet Union in their defeat. In 1994 Reinhold Wagnleitner and Diana M. Wolf published *Coca-Colonization and the Cold War* to illustrate how America's pop culture influx into Austria following the Second World War triggered Austrians to imitate American life; they also note "Hollywood products were an important weapon in the arsenal of the United States" during the ideological fight with the Soviets (Wagnleitner and Wolf, 1994, p.237). This helps explain why Austria, although militarily neutral during the conflict, maintained a capitalist economy while being nearly completely surrounded by communist states or members of the Warsaw Pact.

In addition to pop culture, soft power through the attraction of ideals has also proven to be influential. For example, Joseph Nye has written about China's success with their recent rise of soft power. He notes their entry into the WTO, assistance with the six-party talks on North Korea's nuclear proliferation, and the overall attraction of Chinese culture exhibited by the increasing broadcast coverage of China Radio International and the ever-growing number of tourists who visit the country each year as signs of increased Chinese soft power (Nye 2005). Nye believes this rise in soft power correlates with increased influence; despite the fact the country remains authoritarian. He argues the "Beijing Consensus," the combination of authoritarian government with market economics "has become more popular than the previously dominant Washington Consensus" (Nye 2005). Although the Chinese model may not appear attractive to the United States or Western Europe, Nye contends it has made way in parts of Asia, Africa, and Latin America where semi-authoritarian regimes are trying to develop.

Just as an increased amount of soft power can help a country gain influence on the international stage, a decrease in soft power can have adverse affects. This is evident in the comparison of the coalitions President Bush Sr. and current President George W. Bush were able to construct in each of their American led invasions into Iraq. By consulting foreign heads of state and genuinely respecting multilateral organizations the first President Bush was in the end able to gather a coalition that did not burden the US military as much as the one constructed by his son. In a 2003 interview with John Meacham the elder Bush candidly compared his and his son's efforts by correctively stating, "My coalition-building was far easier"; a keen observation that reflects how soft power has affected influence (Meacham, 2003, p.43).

The Mexican-American War provides an additional example where hard power not supported by soft power can hurt influence. The controversial conflict between the United States and Mexico regarding competing claims to modern-day Texas eventually resulting with Mexico loosing a third of its territory instigated not only over a century of anti-American sentiment, but major difficulties for subsequent US presidents trying to achieve regional influence. For instance, the war caused Mexico to look outward for assistance and security to prevent further US encroachments, such as creating ties with France; thus countering the intentions of the Monroe Doctrine to keep European powers out of New World affairs (Smith, 2000, p.22). Therefore in conclusion, through the Cold War, Chinese, Gulf Wars, and Mexican-American War examples I am confident that soft power plays an intricate role in international influence, and thus when analyzing the Good Neighbor policy and the contra war in Nicaragua I expect to find similar results.

In regards to this project's contribution to academia and the political science discipline it will undoubtedly increase the overall knowledge of the relationship between the United States and Latin America. As lawmakers and political scientists confront the rise of intermestic issues in the American political dialogue, a greater understanding of how to deal with Latin America on the matters of immigration, drug trafficking, and the outsourcing of jobs becomes increasingly crucial.

[...]

Hard Power Is Necessary to Become a Leading State

Allison Fedirka

Allison Fedirka is a senior analyst at Geopolitical Futures.

T he concept of power lies at the center of geopolitics. Power, simply put, is the ability to achieve one's desired outcome. When it comes to countries, the degree of power a country has determines whether it can fulfill its national imperatives—those almost eternal goals that a state cannot help but pursue—or whether it is subordinate to other states.

Many people believe that power can be broken down into two forms: soft power and hard power. Since Joseph Nye popularized the notion of soft power in the early 1990s, it commonly circulates in discussions about international relations. It is typically accompanied by a belief that hard power is a thing of the past (specifically the pre–World War II world) and that states in this "civilized" age engage in diplomacy and trade to get what they want. But some things never change, and there's still no substitute for hard power.

True Strength

Traditionally, hard power includes things like geography, natural resources and military might. Soft power consists of components like technology, education, culture and economic ties. Conceptually, hard power is about coercion, and soft power is about persuasion.

Coercion occurs when country A has enough leverage over the interests of country B to control it—to force it to behave a certain way, even if that means going against country B's will. Take Russia's relationship with Belarus. Russia is the primary supplier of oil and gas to Belarus, which is almost entirely dependent on imports to meet its energy needs. Any time Minsk threatens to act in a way contrary to what Moscow wants, the Kremlin threatens to cut off its energy supplies. Unsurprisingly, Minsk eventually complies, even if that means doing something it doesn't want to do, such as paying higher prices for natural gas imports.

On the other hand, persuasion occurs when country A lacks leverage over country B but still wants country B to behave a certain way. The absence of leverage means country B must decide on its own to comply with country A's desire. This approach is often ineffective because, when there is no pressure to act one way, a country will do whatever is in its best interest, not what is in the interests of someone else. Gestures go only so far. Still, countries engage in soft power strategies because soft power provides a way to potentially achieve an objective at a lower cost than the alternative, and because hard power isn't always an option. The US courting Brazil to enter World War II on the side of the Allies is an example of the first cause, and China's current relationship with the Philippines is an example of the second.

Brazil was neutral for most of World War II. Its government and its people were split on whether to back the US or Germany, and many people don't even realize that Brazil did eventually send troops to Italy to fight for the Allies in the final months of the war. Brazil was of interest to the US because its northern coast would help cement control over the Northern Atlantic and would open up control of the Southern Atlantic. The US soft power campaign consisted of diplomatic visits, trade and cultural exchanges, such as creating films featuring Disney's Ze Carioca (Donald Duck's suave Brazilian counterpart) and Carmen Miranda (the Brazilian bombshell with her own star on the Hollywood Walk of Fame) for consumption in both countries.

The soft power approach gradually swayed Brazil toward the US, culminating in a diplomatic gesture: severing ties with the Axis powers. But Brazil stopped short of declaring war. In response, Germany initiated a submarine campaign targeting Brazilian merchant ships. It sank dozens of ships and cost hundreds of lives.

In the end, it was Germany's hard power response that spurred Brazil to enter the war on the side of the Allies.

A modern-day scenario, and one that shows soft power being used when hard power isn't an option, is China's approach to the Philippines. To guarantee its supply chains and trade routes, China needs direct access to the Pacific Ocean and South China Sea. The islands that make up the Philippines stand in the way of this access, so it is in China's interest to control those islands—or at least to be able to influence the people who control those islands. Complicating matters for China is the fact that the US military is the security guarantor for Pacific water traffic, and the Philippines relies heavily on the US for trade and security cooperation. Though China could overpower the Philippines, it cannot take on the US to win control over the Philippines. Instead, it has resorted to channeling large investments and other trade deals to win over Manila. At best, this may lay the groundwork for future levers over the Philippines, but for now, Manila has decisively sided with the United States, which guarantees its security but does not directly challenge its sovereignty and is a strong economic partner.

Soft Power Doesn't Make Great Powers

Nevertheless, many remain fixated on soft power. Just this week, a U.K.-based consultancy firm called Portland, in cooperation with the USC Center on Public Diplomacy, published a report ranking the world's top 30 countries by soft power. The ranking is based on the composite score of soft power elements: culture, digital footprint, government, engagement, education and business/ enterprise. The first thing that stands out is that European countries dominate the list, and these countries outrank others that are geopolitical heavyweights. Ireland outranks Russia, and Greece is above China. In fact, Russia, China and Turkey are all in the bottom six of this top-30 ranking. That two small European countries are considered more powerful than three much larger countries— countries that are major geopolitical centers of gravity—should automatically raise questions about the credibility of soft power.

A second observation is that most of the countries at the top of the soft power ranking —France, the U.K., the US and Germany —are also among the world leaders in hard power. The US has regularly demonstrated that through hard power measures such as sanctions or military activity, it can coerce other countries to change their behavior. Germany is the economic powerhouse of the European Union and has threatened economic measures against smaller EU countries, especially Greece, to coerce them into supporting EU regulations. France's cultural influence—a component of soft power—does have global reach, but the foundation for this cultural influence was colonization, a product of hard power.

Soft power reads well on paper, but its dependence on persuasion makes it largely inconsequential in the world of geopolitics, whereas hard power dictates reality and the course of events.

Soft Power Cannot Replace Hard Power

Colin S. Gray

Colin S. Gray is a professor of international relations and strategic studies at the University of Reading in the United Kingdom.

[...]

Power is one of the more contestable concepts in political theory, but it is conventional and convenient to define it as "the ability to effect the outcomes you want and, if necessary, to change the behavior of others to make this happen." (Joseph S. Nye, Jr.) In recent decades, scholars and commentators have chosen to distinguish between two kinds of power, "hard" and "soft." The former, hard power, is achieved through military threat or use, and by means of economic menace or reward. The latter, soft power, is the ability to have influence by co-opting others to share some of one's values and, as a consequence, to share some key elements on one's agenda for international order and security. Whereas hard power obliges its addressees to consider their interests in terms mainly of calculable costs and benefits, principally the former, soft power works through the persuasive potency of ideas that foreigners find attractive. The nominal promise in this logic is obvious. Plainly, it is highly desirable if much of the world external to America wants, or can be brought to want, a great deal of what America happens to favor also. Coalitions of the genuinely willing have to be vastly superior to the alternatives.

Unfortunately, although the concept of American soft power is true gold in theory, in practice it is not so valuable. Ironically, the empirical truth behind the attractive concept is just sufficient to mislead policymakers and grand strategists. Not only do Americans want to believe that the soft power of their civilization and culture is truly potent, we are all but programmed by our

"Hard Power and Soft Power: The Utility of Military Force as an Instrument of Policy in the 21st Century," by Colin S. Gray, The Strategic Studies Institute, April 2011.

enculturation to assume that the American story and its values do and should have what amounts to missionary merit that ought to be universal. American culture is so powerful a programmer that it can be difficult for Americans to empathize with, or even understand, the somewhat different values and their implications held deeply abroad. The idea is popular, even possibly authoritative, among Americans that ours is not just an "ordinary country," but instead is a country both exceptionally blessed (by divine intent) and, as a consequence, exceptionally obliged to lead Mankind. When national exceptionalism is not merely a proposition, but is more akin to an iconic item of faith, it is difficult for usually balanced American minds to consider the potential of their soft power without rose-tinted spectacles. And the problem is that they are somewhat correct. American values, broadly speaking "the American way," to hazard a large project in reductionism, are indeed attractive beyond America's frontiers and have some utility for US policy. But there are serious limitations to the worth of the concept of soft power, especially as it might be thought of as an instrument of policy. To date, the idea of soft power has not been subjected to a sufficiently critical forensic examination. In particular, the relation of the soft power of attraction and persuasion to the hard power of coercion urgently requires more rigorous examination than it has received thus far.

When considered closely, the subject of soft power and its implications for the hard power of military force reveals a number of plausible working propositions that have noteworthy meaning for US policy and strategy.

1. Hard military threat and use are more difficult to employ today than was the case in the past, in part because of the relatively recent growth in popular respect for universal humanitarian values. However, this greater difficulty does not mean that military force has lost its distinctive ability to secure some political decisions. The quality of justification required for the use of force has risen, which

means that the policy domain for military relevance has diminished, but has by no means disappeared.

2. The political and other contexts for the use of force today do not offer authoritative guidance for the future. History is not reliably linear. To know the 2000s is not necessarily to know the 2010s.

3. The utility of military force is not a fixed metric value, either universally or for the United States. The utility of force varies with culture and circumstance, *inter alia*. It is not some free-floating objective calculable truth.

4. For both good and for ill, ethical codes are adapted and applied under the pressure of more or less stressful circumstances, and tend to be significantly situational in practice. This is simply the way things are and have always been. What a state licenses or tolerates by way of military behavior effected in its name depends to a degree on how desperate and determined are its policymakers and strategists,

5. War involves warfare, which means military force, which means violence that causes damage, injury, and death. Some of the debate on military force and its control fails to come to grips with the bloody reality, chaos, and friction that is in the very nature of warfare. Worthy and important efforts to limit conduct in warfare cannot avoid accepting the inherent nastiness of the subject. War may be necessary and it should be restrained in its conduct, but withal it is by definition illiberally violent behavior.

6. By and large, soft power should not be thought of as an instrument of policy. America is what it is, and the ability of Washington to project its favored "narrative(s)" is heavily constrained. Cultural diplomacy and the like are hugely mortgaged by foreigners' own assessments of their interests. And a notable dimension of culture is local,

which means that efforts to project American ways risk fueling "blow-back."

7. Soft power cannot sensibly be regarded as a substantial alternative to hard military power. Familiarity with the concept alone encourages the fallacy that hard and soft power have roughly equivalent weight and utility. An illusion of broad policy choice is thus fostered, when in fact effective choices are severely constrained.

8. An important inherent weakness of soft power as an instrument of policy is that it utterly depends upon the uncoerced choices of foreigners. Sometimes their preferences will be compatible with ours, but scarcely less often they will not be. Interests and cultures do differ.

9. Soft power tends to be either so easy to exercise that it is probably in little need of a policy push, being essentially preexistent, or too difficult to achieve because local interests, or culture, or both, deny it political traction.

10. Hard and soft power should be complementary, though often they are not entirely so. US national style, reflecting the full array of American values as a hegemonic power, has been known to give some cultural and hence political offense abroad, even among objective allies and other friends. Whereas competent strategy enables hard military power to be all, or most of what it can be, soft power does not lend itself readily to strategic direction.

11. Provided the different natures of hard and soft power are understood—the critical distinguishing factor being coercion versus attraction—it is appropriate to regard the two kinds of power as mutual enablers. However, theirs is an unequal relationship. The greater attractiveness of soft power is more than offset in political utility by its inherent unsuitability for policy direction and control.

From all the factors above, it follows that military force will long remain an essential instrument of policy. That said, popular enthusiasm in Western societies for the placing of serious restraints on the use of force can threaten the policy utility of the military. The ill consequences of America's much-manifested difficulty in thinking and behaving strategically are augmented perilously when unwarranted faith is placed upon soft power that inherently is resistant to strategic direction. Although it is highly appropriate to be skeptical of the policy utility of soft power, such skepticism must not be interpreted as implicit advice to threaten or resort to military force with scant reference to moral standards. Not only is it right in an absolute sense, it is also expedient to seek, seize, and hold the moral high ground. There can be significant strategic advantage in moral advantage—to risk sounding cynical. Finally, it is essential to recognize that soft power tends to work well when America scarcely has need of it, but the more challenging contexts for national security require the mailed fist, even if it is cushioned, but not concealed, by a glove of political and ethical restraint.

[...]

Force Is Necessary in the Pursuit of Peace

Brad Macdonald

Brad Macdonald is the Europe bureau chief and managing editor for the Trumpet.

Mankind's timeless and dogged pursuit of peace is a tribute to our perseverance and optimism. World leaders dedicate their lives to fostering peace. World organizations such as the United Nations exist to pursue global peace. Countless billions of dollars flow into efforts to quiet the drum of war. When these options fail, nations often seek peace *through war*.

Lasting peace is the ultimate, yet hardest to achieve desire of mankind. History declares the tragic inevitability of war. Every alternative has been tried, every path walked, but we are still no closer to learning the way of lasting peace. Today, though peace has never been more desperately needed, it has never been more elusive.

The Western world, America in particular, has been waging war to achieve peace for half a decade now. Public discussion in the United States rings with calls for an end to war-making and a revival of diplomatic efforts to achieve global aims. *Peace through diplomacy* has become a national catchphrase. Many public figures increasingly play down the need for force or military action, demanding that US foreign policy be reconstructed around rhetoric, conversation—*diplomacy.*

Of course, it is infinitely preferable, whenever possible, to achieve foreign policy objectives through diplomacy. The question is: Is this a time when diplomacy alone can achieve the peace we crave?

It appears the present administration in Washington is coming to believe the answer is yes. After labeling Iran and North Korea

"Peace Through Diplomacy: Can It Work?" by Brad Macdonald, The Trumpet, May 2007. Reprinted by permission.

as members of an axis of evil and Syria a rogue state and long maintaining a policy of refusing to entertain such nations in direct diplomatic talks, the president has lately shown himself willing to sit down with these same nations at a table laid with negotiation and compromise. In March, the US held high-level talks with Iran and Syria on the future of Iraq, and scheduled a follow-up meeting for April. The same month, the assistant secretary of state met with North Korean officials in New York to discuss normalizing relations between their two nations—steps that could include removing North Korea from America's list of state sponsors of terrorism and opening a trading relationship.

As America launches this diplomatic offensive with its enemies—a foreign policy direction likely to be pursued more intensively in coming months and years—it is worth considering the art of diplomacy. What is the key to effective diplomacy? Is the US in a position to employ high-quality diplomacy? More fundamentally, can diplomacy of even the highest quality secure peace in the long term? What *is* the way to lasting peace?

The Art of Diplomacy

Furthering national interest through peaceful means is the ultimate purpose of diplomacy. International relations expert Hans Morgenthau wrote, "Of all the factors that make for the power of a nation, *the most important*, however unstable, *is the quality of diplomacy*" (*Politics Among Nations;* emphasis mine throughout). High-quality diplomacy is one of the strongest weapons a nation can possess. Weak diplomacy, on the other hand, can thrust a nation into crisis.

What will be the quality of America's diplomacy with Iran, Syria and North Korea?

Morgenthau explained diplomacy as the "art of bringing the different elements of the national power to bear with maximum effect upon those points in the international situation which concern the national interest most directly." Effective diplomacy occurs when a government uses the elements of national power at its disposal—its political connections and influence, geographic situation, economic and industrial capacity, military might—to promote its national interests. Intelligent diplomacy, wrote Morgenthau, harnesses these qualities and pursues its objectives by three means: persuasion, compromise, and threat of force.

Effective diplomacy employs the power of persuasion, compromises at the right time and on the right issues, and—when necessary—uses the threat of military force. It requires the careful, well-timed blending of all three of these components.

"Rarely, if ever," Morgenthau wrote, "in the conduct of the foreign policy of a great power is there justification for using only one method to the exclusion of the others." The art of diplomacy consists of placing the right emphasis on each of the three means at its disposal at the right time. "A diplomacy that puts most of its eggs in the basket of compromise when the military might of the nation should be predominantly displayed," for example, "or stresses military might when the political situation calls for persuasion and compromise, will … fail."

Effective diplomacy requires that rhetoric be *underpinned* by military strength. "Diplomacy without arms," as the Prussian king Frederick the Great stated, "is like music without instruments."

The fact is, history shows that unless a credible military option exists, persuasion and compromise have little effect in dealing with hostile regimes. And whether America accepts it or not, Iran, Syria and North Korea are hostile regimes.

A Critical Case Study

Sept. 30, 1938, was a momentous day in the life of Neville Chamberlain. As he stepped onto the tarmac of Heston airport, he could barely contain his excitement. Clasped in his fingers was the fruit of a long process of hard-fought diplomacy. Jubilance filled the air. The sense of relief was palpable. Standing before the eager public, the prime minister considered the significance that history would award this day. Sept. 30, 1938, would be a glorious testament to the power of diplomacy.

It was on this day that Britain's Prime Minister Chamberlain, waving the non-aggression agreement signed by Adolf Hitler, declared those infamous words: "Peace for our time." During the conference in Munich, the power of rhetoric had prevailed and the clenched fist of war was thwarted.

Or so it seemed.

Less than a year later, Hitler flouted the non-aggression pact, fired up the engines of his military, and ignited World War II by rumbling eastward into Poland. France and Britain declared war on Germany, and Chamberlain's diplomacy was officially pronounced dead.

It is critical we consider the history of pre–World War II diplomacy in the context of current events, and how American leaders are handling global challenges.

The story of the 1930s is of the *failure* of diplomacy because Britain did not demonstrate it was prepared to take action. Hitler laughed at the agreement because he knew Britain was not arming for war; he didn't believe there would be consequences for breaking the agreement he had signed. What's more, Britain had a *track record* of *ignoring* Germany's aggression. When German troops occupied the demilitarized zone of the Rhineland in 1936, Britain did nothing. When Hitler ordered his troops into Austria in March 1938, there was no reaction. And with the Munich Pact itself relinquishing Czechoslovakia's Sudeten territory to Germany, what possible incentive did Hitler have to halt his campaign to take over Europe? Diplomacy was *rewarding* his aggression.

Compare this with what is happening today with the US. Notice this opinion piece from Novosti, a Russian news agency: "This about-face [embracing hostile nations in diplomatic talks] of American diplomacy is all the more astounding since it took place in a matter of a month and a half. In middle January Condoleezza Rice reassured the Senate that the United States would not go for any bilateral diplomatic contacts with North Korea, Iran or Syria until they became reasonably flexible on disputable issues. The

US secretary of state described the policies of these countries as 'extortion' rather than diplomacy.

This 'extortion' is still in place, and it is Washington that has become flexible ... Nobody could match Rice in the UN Security Council in her demands for tough sanctions against North Korea after its nuclear test in October. In the case of Iran and Syria, she also preceded the invitation to the conference in Baghdad with a package of confrontation-provoking speeches, and accused Tehran of collaboration with the Shiite militants in attacking US troops. *To sum up, each time dessert followed the bitter pill"* (March 6).

The parallels with British diplomacy in the 1930s are disconcerting. Like Britain's pre–World War II appeasement and non-action, the US's track record instills no fear into rogue nations. For example, bombings of US interests in Saudi Arabia, Kenya and Tanzania during the '90s met with virtually no response. After maintaining that North Korean nuclear capability would not be tolerated, the US took no action when Pyongyang exploded its first nuclear bomb in a test last October. Iran's ongoing support of terrorists, incitement of violence in Iraq, and pursuit of nuclear capability provoke little real action from the US.

Also degrading the deterrent capability of America's military threat is the nation's history of exiting a war theater once things get tough. America's enemies have witnessed hasty retreats from Vietnam and Somalia, and are watching Iraq. In addition, antiwar Democrats and the mainstream media are playing a powerful part in undermining any threat of military force. Other nations know America's government is isolated and would become even more so if it resorted to force against Iran, North Korea or Syria.

This all raises the question: As America begins to engage its enemies diplomatically, does it have a credible threat of military force? If not, then we can predict that its diplomatic efforts with

Iran, Syria and North Korea will crumble and that violence and conflict will eventually prevail.

Unfortunately, it appears this is essentially the situation as it stands. In its enemies' eyes, the use of force by America is extremely unlikely, hence rendering US diplomacy largely ineffective.

Another Case Study

Theodore Roosevelt was the first US president to see that America had the potential to be a world power. He knew that effective diplomacy was key to realizing this potential—and that threat of action was an indispensable component of it.

Speaking at the Naval War College in Newport on June 2, 1897, Roosevelt said, "Diplomacy is utterly useless when there is no force behind it. The diplomat is the servant, not the master, of the soldier. There are higher things in this life than the soft and easy enjoyment of material comfort. It is through strife, or the readiness for strife, that a nation must win greatness." He made that comment at the dawn of American greatness.

The truth of his statement has never been more evident than in our danger-fraught world.

Iran, Syria and North Korea have a history of exploiting concessions, rejecting agreements and trampling on other nations' willingness to compromise. Though America may come away from diplomatic talks with agreements in hand, what will it do if and when Iran or North Korea refuses to meet their agreements? If these countries are confident that the US is not prepared to back up its compromise and persuasion with meaningful military action, how effective will the diplomacy be?

Entering into a diplomatic relationship with these nations will be a litmus test of the strength of the US government. Will diplomacy further America's national interest and secure a measure of peace? Or will it only serve to promote the interests of these rogue states and further ruin America's power and reputation?

Gathering Dangers

Seventeenth-century English historian Thomas Fuller said, "[I]t is madness for sheep to talk peace with a wolf."

The Middle East seethes with problems for America right now. Israel faces the possibility of a three-front war with Syria in the Golan Heights, Hezbollah in Lebanon, and Hamas in the Gaza Strip. Syria and Iran are pushing for the downfall of the moderate, US-friendly government of Lebanon. Iraq quakes with civil strife between the government and several competing militias. Like Germany in the 1930s, every sign says war is only getting worse across the Middle East.

How does America respond to these clear and present dangers? *Yank the troops out, and let's sit down at the negotiating table with Iran and Syria.* Many American and British leaders, like Chamberlain, are sheep seeking negotiation with wolves.

The tragic result of such weak diplomacy is that we are moving into an era when the enemies of Western civilization simply *do not fear consequences* for their actions. Hence, Hezbollah starts a war against Israel; Hamas continues to launch missiles onto Israeli soil; North Korea tests long-range missiles and nuclear weapons; Iran continues to threaten to do the same; Iraqi and Afghan insurgents brazenly attack Western forces.

Increasingly, America's enemies have no fear!

On that day in 1938, Chamberlain's style of diplomacy strengthened the enemy and precipitated conflict. The only thing Chamberlain secured for the Continent was *time*: The people had 11 more months of relative peace—while Hitler had 11 more months of preparation—followed by a bloody and lethal war.

This perfectly illustrates the futility of diplomacy if a nation is *weak* and unprepared to *back up* its words. "Diplomacy without a realistic threat of significant action, in the event that diplomacy fails," said Dr. George Friedman from Stratfor Systems, "*is just empty chatter*." That statement summarizes American foreign policy today. When it comes to problems such as Iran's involvement in Iraq, the policy of the American government is little more than *empty chatter*—conversations not underpinned by *action*. Thus, the diplomacy may buy some time, but the time will serve only the *aggressor*, not America.

[...]

CHAPTER 3

Has Social Media Had a Positive Influence on Diplomacy?

Social Media Is a New Frontier for Public Diplomacy

Clifton Martin and Laura Jagla

Laura Jagla is a communications specialist with USAID. Clifton Martin is a Foreign Service officer in the US State Department.

I n the period leading up to the overthrow of political authorities in the Middle East, young activists used social media to spread dissident discourse, organize protests and transmit live footage of revolutions across the world. Simultaneously, stubborn autocrats clung to political survival tactics by blocking their citizens' access to social media sites like Twitter and Facebook in order to disrupt the gathering momentum of a networked people determined to change their governments.

As many scholars and practitioners will argue, social media was not the deciding force of these revolutionary movements—but they were a key factor. During the 2010 Egyptian uprising in Tahrir Square, masses of people—primarily youth and young adults— organized through Facebook and other social media platforms to protest their government's action or inaction on issues that mattered to them, starting the most powerful Arab political movement of this century. Well before the Tahrir Square protests, similar movements employing social media to protest political leadership had taken place in the Philippines, Iran, Belarus and Thailand.[1] These cases reflect the social composition and choice media options of today's generation. Sociological shifts in demographics and power, which have coincided with increased use of social media, have resulted in movement-making with dramatic political implications. With that background, this report will explore the implication of new technology, particularly social media, on the conduct of American public diplomacy.

"Integrating Diplomacy and Social Media," by Clifton Martin and Laura Jagla, The Aspen Institute, March 2013. Reprinted by permission.

A New World: The International Impact of Social Media

The Aspen Institute Communications and Society Program convened its first annual Aspen Institute Dialogue on Diplomacy and Technology (ADDTech) to create an open dialogue on the evolution of traditional diplomacy in the twenty-first century. Has traditional diplomacy become obsolete in the wake of the current communications advancement? How can a new generation of diplomats across sectors—citizens, corporations and states—use new communications tools to advance their nation's interests? What institutions should be responsible for managing 21st Century Statecraft? A variant of this discussion is taking place in every government on this planet. It is new to everyone no matter the age.

The purpose of diplomacy is to promote the interests of the state within the international system. The US government's top national security priority, according to many veteran diplomats, is to advance the interests of the United States within a world made more stable by effective and democratic governance. In the new era, policymakers will need to recognize that progress toward this goal will be affected not only by what other governments do, but also by the interconnected social networks of global citizens. To get their messages across, American leaders will need to speak directly to all people.

According to the White House's 2012 "Update to Congress on National Framework for Strategic Communication," executive leadership has laid out the framework for interdepartmental cooperation in communication strategy. Alec Ross, Senior Advisor for Innovation in the Office of the Secretary at the US Department of State, emphasized at the Dialogue that the US State Department has become a frontrunner for employing technology in diplomatic engagement. Two years prior, the "Quadrennial Diplomacy and Development Review" (QDDR) set forth initiatives in influencing public opinion, opening economic possibilities and engaging women in the public sector through the tools of technology. With people worldwide sharing information easily and rapidly through communication technology, Ross emphasized, the State Department needs to stay ahead of the game and "know about the revolution before everyone else knows about it."

While the US Department of State leads significant government innovation in the domain of technology and diplomacy, policy and strategy on engagement and communications with other countries is not limited to this department. Various other government entities and agencies contribute to developments in this field including the Department of Defense (DOD), the Intelligence Community (IC) and the Broadcasting Board of Governors (BBG).[2] Interagency planning and coordination has been particularly useful in US government efforts to achieve its strategic goals.

Despite this interagency cooperation, ADDTech participants questioned the US government's commitment to technological transformation. While Ross stressed the State Department's strides to incorporate technology into the diplomatic realm, others addressed the oft-adversarial balance between traditional diplomacy and the technological domain. Several insisted that the "communication revolution" calls for leadership in Washington to reconsider traditional diplomacy to incorporate the new technologies, while others argued that tools cannot replace the formalized human diplomatic engagement.

Several participants suggested that while sitting face-to-face takes time and effort, it is historically successful. The State Department may need to incorporate the tools of technology effectively, but it should not forego the rules, strategy and successes of traditional diplomacy. As ADDTech participant Ambassador Christopher Hill, Dean of the University of Denver's Josef Korbel School of International Studies, attested, "The Internet is not always a good space for compromise."

While the tools of technology cannot replace certain aspects of diplomatic engagement, Tamara Cofman-Wittes, Director of the Saban Center for Middle East Policy at the Brookings Institution, voiced her concern that the government may need more of an investment to make a transition to this new world of pervasive technology. Although the US government has prioritized technology across key agencies in supporting global communication and policy, additional investment would help greatly to advance its commitment to and use of communications technology. Indeed, new technological tools lead to disruptions in government structures. The US government and governments across the world will need to adapt to these new challenges.

[...]

References

1. Clay Shirky, "The Political Power of Social Media: Technology, the Public Sphere, and Political Change," *Foreign Affairs*, January/February 2011: 1–2.

2. The White House, "National Framework for Strategic Communication," March 2012, 4. Available online: http://mountainrunner.us/files/2012/03/President -response-to-NDAA- 1055-of-2009.pdf.

Social Media Opens Opportunities for US–Middle Eastern Relations

William Rugh

William Rugh is the Edward R. Murrow Visiting Professor of Public Diplomacy at Tufts University's Fletcher School of Law and Diplomacy and a former ambassador to Yemen and the United Arab Emirates.

The term "soft power" that Harvard Professor Joseph Nye coined is a valuable concept if correctly understood. Nye defined soft power as a nation's power of attraction, in contrast to the hard power of coercion inherent in military or economic strength (Nye, 1990, 2003, 2004a, b). He said soft power derives from a nation's culture, its political values and its foreign policy. Since World War Two, foreign perceptions of the United States have become influenced by its soft power more than ever before. That is partly because the digital communications revolution has made the world more aware of what is happening in America. But Nye explained that soft power attributes can be seen as negative or positive, depending on the perception of the viewer. The digital revolution has made better known to foreign audiences not only America's positive aspects but also some of its negatives ones (Nye, 2003; Compass, 2004b).

"Public diplomacy" is not the same as soft power, although some people, including the Undersecretary for Public Diplomacy, have confused the two terms (Stengel, 2014). Public diplomacy is a deliberate communication effort that makes use of soft power by providing information and examples of aspects of a nation's soft power that are regarded by a foreign audience as positive. In the case of American public diplomacy, the US government uses a

"American Soft Power and Public Diplomacy in the Arab World," by William Rugh, Springer Nature, January 10, 2017. https://www.nature.com/articles/palcomms2016104. Licensed under CC BY 4.0.

variety of different ways to do that. These include sending American musicians, theatre groups, art and photographic collections, and speakers abroad, to demonstrate aspects of American culture. American public diplomacy soft power objectives are also supported by American libraries, book programs abroad and book translations as well as exchange programs that bring foreign students and professionals to the United States to see for themselves aspects of American society and culture. English teaching programs abroad, promoted as part of a US public diplomacy effort, especially those taught by American citizens, also help convey aspects of American society and culture (Rugh, 2014: Chapter 8–10). All of these programs are designed to present aspects of soft power that serve to attract foreign audiences.

This study will examine the role of America's soft power in the Arab world. It will look at the dissemination of soft power products in that region by the US government as part of an official public diplomacy programme. It will also discuss how public diplomacy officers face those challenges and make use of soft power. But this study will also help shed light on the broader question of whether American power in the world, including soft power, has declined, a question that is being debated by scholars.

Public Diplomacy and Soft Power in the Arab World

Since [World] War II, the US government has systematically sought to make use of soft power in the Arab world, using a variety of means to reach those audiences (Rugh, 2006). It has sought to counteract or put into context the negative stories, and it has sought to reinforce the positive aspects of American soft power by using all of the public diplomacy tools available. Making use of American soft power has always been a central element of US public diplomacy efforts in the Arab world, but changes in the working environment have led to changes in the approach. The following are some of the major current challenges that US public diplomacy professionals face in communicating with Arab audiences.

Can we generalize about the Arabs? There are approximately 350 million people in the Middle East and North Africa who can be called Arabs because Arabic is their mother tongue. But they tend to have a wide range of attitudes and affiliations, depending partly on whether they are Sunni, Shia or Christian; wealthy to poor; urban or rural, and so on. Yet they have much in common, and generalizations are possible, so it is common for respectable scholars to refer in their publications to "Arab attitudes" or "Arab perceptions" (Telhami, Cole, and Nakhleh).

One challenge in writing about Arab public opinion is the scarcity of reliable polling data. Until two decades ago Arab polls were almost nonexistent because of Arab government restrictions, but today researchers like John Zogby, Shibley Telhami and the Gallup Organization are able to carry out regular polling in some Arab countries. American diplomats and intelligence officers have, however, collected a great deal of empirical data, mostly non-statistical, about Arab views, and if they have served in the region for any length of time and have engaged with Arabs on a daily basis, they are able to compile a reasonably accurate picture—although incomplete—of how Arabs think. The present author spent fifty years working in and on the Arab world and as a result has some sense of Arab attitudes.

The basic fact that every American diplomat who has served in the Arab world knows is this: most Arabs are critical or highly critical of aspects of American foreign policy toward the region, yet at the same time they tend to hold very positive views of the United States as a country. One opinion poll taken in June 2004 in Morocco, Jordan and the UAE for example, revealed that the public in these countries had favourable opinions about American science and technology (90, 83 and 84%, respectively), US products (73, 61 and 63%), education (61, 59 and 63%), movies and television (60, 56 and 52%), freedom and democracy (53, 57 and 39%), and the American people (59, 52 and 46%). However, this same poll showed that these publics had unfavourable views of US policies toward the Arabs (90, 89 and 87%), toward the Palestinians (93, 89 and

90%), toward Iraq (98, 78 and 91%), and on terrorism (82, 75 and 84%) (Rugh, 2006). Opinion research in 2010 in six Arab countries (Egypt, Jordan, Saudi, Lebanon, Morocco and UAE) found that 76% watched US or European movies 3-7 times weekly, and as many as 47% watched them daily. The United States ranked second highest only behind France for country that supports freedom and democracy, but the United States ranked second (behind Israel 77% and 88%) among countries perceived as posing the biggest threat to the Mideast (Zogby and Maryland, 2010).

The Impact of Digital Age Communication

Greater Competition for US Government Communicators

Before the emergence of modern information technologies, the US government had much greater means of communicating with foreign audiences than it does today. Shortly after World War II, the State Department had not only telegraphic contact with every US embassy abroad, but it also used the so-called "wireless file" to transmit full texts of unclassified policy statements and USG commentaries to every embassy. US diplomats made extensive use of these materials by providing them to local media editors and reporters, and embassy officers also translated official documents into local languages.

Local media found these materials valuable because they usually arrived before the regular news reports about US policy, and translations saved them time and effort. At the same time, the Voice of America was broadcasting every day, in English and in foreign languages, carrying US policy statements—including live transmissions from officials—and commentaries explaining the US government's point of view, as well as accurate information about American society and culture. These services were very useful to the embassy because the local media otherwise received brief wire service versions of the policy statements that had often been distorted by going through that filter. The local media therefore had a more reliable version of the official US statements, and the commentaries provided explanations of US policies and put the statements into context that was helpful to the United States. This enhanced the possibility that the editors and reporters would regard the US policy statements as positive.

Today, however, because of the communications revolution, editors and reporters at foreign newspapers receive information about US policy statements as soon as they are made, through the internet, cell phones and other digital technology that did not exist only a few decades ago. Likewise, events in the United States that can influence foreign perceptions of America one way or another, are now described to foreign audiences much more quickly than ever before, by various private means not controlled by the US government. Foreign audiences no longer need the information from the embassy as they once did. As a result, they no longer see full texts of official US policy statements or reports of American developments. They usually do not see full explanations by US officials of what the policy means, or an explanation of developments in American society. In fact, if the means of delivery of these materials are biased or distorted, the local media will receive a biased or distorted version of US policy and society, and that bias often carries a negative spin. Therefore the potential positive impact of the soft power of a US policy statement can be lost because some source other than the US government is providing it.

Public diplomacy professionals at US embassies abroad and at the State Department have joined the twenty-first century international dialogue via new electronic devices, to remain competitive in the effort to reach foreign audiences. They have established websites, personal Twitter accounts, and used YouTube and many other new communication channels to convey aspects of positive soft power to foreign audiences. They make use of the "Rapid Response" bulletin created during the presidency of George W. Bush by his Undersecretary of State for Public Diplomacy and Public Affairs, Karen Hughes, which is intended to help American officials compete with the private sector by providing them with a source of reliable information that is delivered very quickly and in useable form. This bulletin that is sent daily to every embassy is a two or three page paper summarizing foreign comment on the most urgent one or two issues of the day, alongside current US official statements on them. American diplomats use this handy summary of key points to make in their discussions locally. But it is up to them to identify the problem areas in local discussions and use these materials effectively.

US government broadcasting is also still helpful in supplementing the embassy's effort to disseminate information abroad about America. However, for the Arab world, the effectiveness of this tool was diminished during the administration of George W. Bush when Congress passed a law putting the Voice of America and other broadcast channels under a separate Broadcasting Board of Governors (BBG), because the BBG then cancelled the Arabic Service of the VOA, that had been a very effective means to reach audiences in the Arab world. In its place, the BBG created *Sawt al Arab* radio and *al Hurra Television*, both in Arabic, which were intended to be helpful with Arab audiences. However both of them were badly managed and many regular Arab listeners to US government broadcasting were lost (USC Centre and Rugh, 2006: 177).

US public diplomacy officers are therefore making use of the new social media tools that have become ubiquitous, and broadcasting still exists. But they have also found that a proactive effort to engage directly with key members of their local audience remains a vital part of the public diplomacy effort. In one-on-one conversations, US diplomats engage with them to explain American foreign policy and society. Soft power can be used effectively one-on-one. In short, US public diplomacy has met the challenge of the new media by making use of it, but also continuing to use traditional public diplomacy tools such as broadcasting and personal contact that are still effective.

[...]

Social Media Is an Important Tool for Public Diplomacy

Constance Duncombe

Constance Duncombe is a researcher and lecturer at Monash University in Australia.

O n 12 January 2016 two US Navy patrol boats wandered into Iranian waters in the Persian Gulf. Iranian military forces detained the ten mariners on board on Farsi Island. Parallels were quickly drawn between Iranian actions in this instance and the similar episode in 2007 when British sailors and marines entering Iranian waters were detained for over two weeks.[1] A swift resolution seemed extremely unlikely, particularly given an incident in December 2015 when an Iranian military vessel fired on a number of ships including a US aircraft carrier and destroyer.[2]

Yet, remarkably, by the next morning Iran had released the two vessels and their crews. While some suggested the quick resolution was due to gains made through US President Obama's strategy of engagement with Iran, others such as Senator John McCain suggested that such an inference was "ludicrous" and that the "administration's craven desire to preserve the dangerous Iranian deal at all costs evidently knows no limit."[3] Regardless of opinion on how it came about, the swift and peaceful solution to the intrusion into Iranian sovereign territory by US sailors came as a surprise to many. Even Secretary of State John Kerry, himself a key figure in diplomatic efforts to secure the release of the mariners, alluded to the unprecedented nature of Iran's decision, stating: "We can all imagine how a similar situation might have played out three or four years ago."[4] Kerry and his counterpart in Tehran, Iranian Foreign Minister Javad Zarif, were central to the surprising release

"Twitter and Transformative Diplomacy: Social Media and Iran-US Relations," by Constance Duncombe, Oxford University Press. By permission of Oxford University Press.

of the US sailors, speaking on the phone at least five times in the hours immediately following the incident and announcing the successful outcome on Twitter. Kerry posted that the "peaceful and efficient resolution of this issue is a testament to the critical role diplomacy plays in keeping our country secure and strong," while half an hour later Zarif stated that he was "happy to see dialog and respect, not threats and impetuousness, swiftly resolved the #sailors episode. Let's learn from this latest example."[5]

These exchanges are significant because they illustrate vividly the growing role Twitter has come to play in contemporary diplomacy. Not only was Twitter used to communicate the positive outcome; the ability of Kerry and Zarif to communicate so freely—a "relatively new" but "extraordinarily important" situation[6]—is arguably the result of a relationship built through both personal interaction and sustained Twitter communication during the P5+1 nuclear negotiations between 2013 and 2015. Given the difficulties of high-level diplomatic interaction between Iran and the United States since the severing of diplomatic ties in 1980, social media have become a significant platform on which diplomats can communicate.

Social media are thus changing the space within which diplomacy unfolds. Yet diplomacy in all its complexities continues to be perceived as grounded in personal interaction. Recently the renaissance of diplomacy as an academic subject has seen an increase in studies on its practices and the competing roles of structure and agency in its culture and traditions, exploring the pivotal role of political leadership in reaching diplomatic breakthroughs.[7] Important contributions from neuroscience suggest how we can understand this "mind–body and ideational–materialist divide."[8] Yet these analyses concentrate on the individual and interpersonal aspects of diplomacy, rather than exploring the new technology through which diplomacy unfolds. An emerging body of work contributes to understanding the powerful role of technology in world affairs by positioning cyberspace as the new frontier of warfare, identifying technological dimensions of threats to security moving beyond terrorism and into the realm of governance.[9] Other scholars have ventured beyond the idea of technology challenging state sovereignty to examine the power of social media in contemporary statecraft, in what they term "e-diplomacy" and "digital diplomacy."[10] Nevertheless, in focusing on social media and public diplomacy such studies give only very limited attention to the tools diplomats employ in their day-to-day engagement with their counterparts.

The question of how social media facilitate interstate dialogue has not yet been given sufficient attention. There is also a corresponding dearth of empirical studies on this issue, despite a growing policy focus on digital diplomacy. Two questions arise here. First, how effective are social media in developing interpersonal trust between individual diplomatic counterparts? Second, can this medium be an effective platform for dialogue when traditional face-to-face diplomacy is difficult? Understanding the increasingly prominent and powerful, yet largely unknown, variable of social media as a tool of diplomatic practice provides insight into the recurrent question of how diplomats effect change beyond upholding the status quo in the international order.

If diplomacy is the "art of communication,"[11] then Twitter is another platform for dialogue between states. Yet this technology challenges traditional notions of diplomacy according to which it occurs through formal channels of communication and informal face-to-face social engagements. Diplomats are increasingly relying on Twitter in their daily practice to communicate with their counterparts. These exchanges occur in front of a global audience, providing an added level of scrutiny that is unique to this form of communication.

This article seeks to fill a gap in the study of digital diplomacy by examining how Iranian Twitter posts in the lead-up to the 2015 nuclear deal helped Iran to indicate its intention to work towards a positive outcome, an intention that was key to the successful implementation of the Joint Comprehensive Plan of Action (JCPOA). Previous work on the Iranian nuclear issue has shown how openings towards *rapprochement* were closed off by political and security considerations on both sides. For instance, the call by former Iranian President Khatami for a "dialogue of civilizations" corresponded with the relaxation of US sanctions against Iran under the Clinton administration. However, a few years afterwards, and despite Iranian expressions of sympathy following the terrorist attacks of 9/11, the Bush administration labelled Iran as part of the "axis of evil," prompting Iran to invest massively in its nuclear programme and triggering wide-ranging concerns in the West as to the true nature and purpose of its development. From 2002, when the existence of a heavy water reactor in Arak and a uranium enrichment plant in Nantaz were first publicized, until 2013, both the Bush and the Obama administrations followed the "basic American formula for dealing with Iran since 1979":[12] that is, attempts to curtail Iran's development of its nuclear programme, involving various "sabre-rattling" threats of military invasion or statements of "official reluctance to contemplate such an outcome," and the imposition of increasingly harsh US and UN sanctions against Iran, with limited success.[13]

Explanations of Iran's agreement to the surprisingly successful JCPOA suggest that Tehran's strategy of nuclear hedging ultimately reached the limits of the state's feasible development of its nuclear programme.[14] A key component of these analyses concerns Iranian identity and how this has influenced its hedging strategy and stance of nuclear defiance.[15] Core aspects of Iranian identity are well understood—its desire for independence, perception of justice and resistance to western dominance, and the interplay of Persian heritage and revolutionary Shi'ism.[16] Iran effectively integrated the dual-track strategy employed by the United States into its self-image of resistance to western interference and strengthened sovereign independence and progress.[17] The question arises here of how, given the strong ideational character and domestic popularity of its nuclear stance, Iran came to agree to the JCPOA. Nevertheless, concern has continued to focus on how to contain Iran at a sufficiently low level of latency, minimizing hedging risks and regional proliferation, rather than turning to examine what precisely has changed on the Iranian side to allow this agreement to come to fruition.[18]

I argue that the role of Twitter as a key part of negotiating strategy is a crucial demonstration of how social media can shape the struggle for recognition, and thereby legitimize political possibilities for change. Recognition provides a positive affirmation of identity that maintains an actor's self-esteem.[19] Our identity is formed through reflexive patterns of how others recognize us. When a state believes it is recognized in a way that is different from how it represents itself, it may engage in a "struggle for recognition" to convince others it should be represented, and recognized, in a diferent way.[20] Social media are implicated in this intersubjective policy–identity process. Facebook, Twitter and Instagram, among other user-generated sites, effectively "cultivate communities of identity performance that reaffirm more than question" the parameters of state identity.[21] Statements made on social media can reflect "us and them" demarcations, framing state identity and difference and a state's desire for recognition from others. How a state represents itself and recognizes others via social media can make particular foreign policy options possible and rule out others.

If we are attuned to shifts in representational patterns communicated through Twitter during high-level negotiations as part of the struggle for recognition, we can also ascertain political possibilities for change earlier than might normally be the case. Prior to the advent of social media, diplomacy largely enjoyed a "cushion of time" between manoeuvre and response.[22] The collapse of space and time brought about by these new channels of instant communication has added to the complex environment in which diplomacy occurs. Contemporary diplomacy is characterized by greater frequency of communication and wider dispersal of information through social media. Diplomats and political leaders will often have limited time to digest and evaluate information posted on social media.[23] What results is a slow realization of change, as the nuances of social media communication may be overlooked due to time constraints.[24] Yet if Twitter posts are examined closely as another vehicle for information in addition to official policy statements, we can begin to see how possible openings for dialogue have formed over time.

[...]

Notes

1. David E. Sanger, Eric Schmitt and Helene Cooper, "Iran's Swift Release of US Sailors Hailed as a Sign of Warmer Relations," *New York Times*, 13 Jan. 2016, http://www.nytimes.com/2016/01/14/world/middleeast/iran-navy -crew-release.html?action=click&contentCollection=Middle%20 East&module=RelatedCoverage&region=En dOfArticle&pgtype=article. (Unless otherwise noted at point of citation, all URLs cited in this article were accessible on 16 Feb. 2017.)

2. *Guardian*, "US Accuses Iran of Conducting 'Highly Provocative' Rocket Test Near Warships," 30 Dec. 2015, https://www.theguardian.com/world/2015/dec/30/us -accuses-iran-of-conducting-highly-provocative-rocket-test-near-warships.

3. McCain quoted in Sanger et al., "Iran's Swift Release."

4. "Iran's Revolutionary Guards Release 10 US Sailors Detained After Straying into Territorial Waters," ABC News, 14 Jan. 2016, http://www.abc.net.au/news/2016 -01-13/iran-revoluntionary-guards-release-us-sailors/7087470.

5. "Iran's Revolutionary Guards."

6. Sanger et al., "Iran's Swift Release."

7. Marcus Holmes, "Diplomacy After Policy-Making: Theorizing Hyper-empowered Individuals," *International Studies Review* 17: 4, 2015, p. 708.

8. Marcus Holmes, "International Politics at the Brain's Edge: Social Neuroscience and a New 'Via Media,'" *International Studies Perspectives* 15: 2, 2014, p. 221; Jonathan Mercer, "Emotional Beliefs," *International Organization* 64: 1, 2010, pp. 1–31.

9. Julien Nocetti, "Contest and Conquest: Russia and Global Internet Governance," *International Affairs* 91: 1, Jan. 10 2015, pp. 111–30; Rex Hughes, "A Treaty for Cyberspace," *International Affairs* 86: 2, March 2010, pp. 523–41.

10. Philip Seib, *Real-Time Diplomacy: Politics and Power in the Social Media Era* (New York: Palgrave Macmillan, 2012); Corneliu Bjola and Marcus Holmes, *Digital Diplomacy: Theory and Practice* (London: Routledge, 2015); Corneliu Bjola and Markus Kornprobst, *Understanding International Diplomacy: Theory, Practice and Ethics* (London: Routledge, 2015), pp. 161–5; Nigel Gould-Davies, "Review Article: The Intimate Dance of Diplomacy: In Praise of Practice," *International Affairs* 89: 6, Nov. 2013, p. 1464.

11. Nicholas J. Wheeler, "Investigating Diplomatic Transformations," *International Affairs* 89: 2, March 2013, p. 477.

12. Ray Takeyh and Suzanne Maloney, "The Self-Limiting Success of Iran Sanctions," *International Affairs* 87: 6, Nov. 2011, p. 1298.

13. Wyn Q. Bowen and Joanna Kidd, "The Iranian Nuclear Challenge," *International Affairs* 80: 2, March 2004, pp. 257–76; Adam Quinn, "The Art of Declining Politely: Obama's Prudent Presidency and the Waning of American Power," *International Affairs* 87: 4, July 2011, pp. 817–18; Wyn Q. Bowen and Jonathan Brewer, "Iran's Nuclear Challenge: Nine Years and Counting," *International* Affairs 87: 4, July 2011, pp. 923–43.

14. Wyn Bowen and Matthew Moran, "Living with Nuclear Hedging: The Implications of Iran's Nuclear Strategy," *International Affairs* 91: 4, July 2015, pp. 687–707.

15. Wade L. Huntley, "Rebels Without a Cause: North Korea, Iran and the NPT," *International Affairs* 82: 4, July 16 2006, p. 735.

16. See Constance Duncombe, "Representation, Recognition and Foreign Policy in the Iran–US Relationship," *European Journal of International Relations* 22: 3, 2016, pp. 622–45; Manuchehr Sanadjian, "Nuclear Fetishism, the Fear of the 'Islamic' Bomb and National Identity in Iran," *Social Identities* 14: 1, 2008, pp. 77–100.

17. Takeyh and Maloney, "The Self-Limiting Success of Iran Sanctions," p. 1306; Dina Esfandiary and Arine Taba-tabai, "Iran's ISIS Policy," *International Affairs* 91: 1, Jan. 2015, p. 11.

18. Bowen and Moran, "Living with Nuclear Hedging"; Huntley, "Rebels Without a Cause."

19. Duncombe, "Representation, Recognition and Foreign Policy."

20. Duncombe, "Representation, Recognition and Foreign Policy"; Erik Ringmar, "Performing International Systems: Two East-Asian Alternatives to the Westphalian Order," *International Organization* 66: 1, 2012, pp. 1–25.

21. Craig Hayden, Don Waisanen and Yelena Osipova, "Facilitating the Conversation: The 2012 Presidential Election and the Public Diplomacy of US Social Media," *American Behavioral Scientist* 57: 11, 2013, p. 1635.

22. Seib, *Real-Time Diplomacy*, p. 86.

23. Seib, *Real-Time Diplomacy*, p. 6.

24. Seib, *Real-Time Diplomacy*, p. 6.

Social Media Undermines Diplomacy

Luis Gómez Romero

Luis Gómez Romero is a senior lecturer in human rights, constitutional law, and legal theory at the University of Wollongong in Australia.

Six days after taking office, President Donald Trump is facing the first international crisis of his administration. And it's unfolding on Twitter.

Following through on campaign promises to crack down on immigration, Trump signed executive orders to both kick-start the construction of a border wall with Mexico and block federal grants for "sanctuary cities"—jurisdictions that offer safe harbour for undocumented immigrants.

Trump justified these measures as necessary for improving domestic security. "A nation without borders is not a nation," he said. "Beginning today, the United States of America gets back control of its borders."

After signing the orders, Trump insisted in an interview with ABC news network that Mexico would reimburse construction expenses "at a later date."

Trump's push to force Mexico to pay for the wall has plunged the two neighbours into a tense and unusual diplomatic standoff. Mexico has long been a key partner and ally of the US and Enrique Peña Nieto's government has keenly tried to avoid a standoff. Trump, on the other hand, has fuelled one with his frantic social media activity.

Welcome to the era of Twitter diplomacy.

"Twitter Diplomacy: How Trump Is Using Social Media to Spur a Crisis with Mexico," by Luis Gómez Romero, The Conversation, January 28, 2017. https://theconversation.com/twitter-diplomacy-how-trump-is-using-social-media-to-spur-a-crisis-with-mexico-71981. Licensed under CC BY-ND 4.0.

American Non-diplomacy

Historically, diplomacy is not one of America's strong suits. Former UN Secretary General Boutros Boutros-Ghali once noted that he was surprised to learn that US international officials usually see "little need for diplomacy." For Americans, Boutros-Ghali claimed, it's perceived as "a waste of time and prestige and a sign of weakness."

But with Mexico President Trump has taken this tradition of American non-diplomacy to uncharted territories.

Peña Nieto chose moderation and diplomatic subtlety to address Trump's belligerence. This conciliatory strategy has, indeed, been perceived as a sign of weakness on both sides of the border.

Yet the Mexican government's situation is delicate. Either Peña Nieto endures Trump's relentless humiliation, or he jeopardises the nation's commercial partnership with the US, which buys 80% of Mexican exports.

So Peña Nieto did everything possible to appease Trump, probably hoping that he would eventually moderate his positions. He even appointed Luis Videgaray—the unpopular politician who organised then-candidate Trump's ill-received August 2016 visit to Mexico—as Minister of Foreign Relations.

Trump answered the conciliatory gesture, which was deeply controversial in Mexico, by tweeting that his southern neighbours would pay for the wall in the border "a little later" in order to build it "more quickly."

Peña Nieto then tried to warn Trump about the consequences that a conflict with Mexico could have upon the US agenda. Using the infamous druglord Joaquín Guzmán Loera, aka El Chapo, as a subtle rebuke to Trump's stance on Mexico, the president extradited him to the US on January 19, just a few hours before Barack Obama's term expired.

US officials and the Mexican public interpreted the timing of the extradition, which had been green-lighted for months, as a Mexican housewarming gift to the Trump White House.

But a different hypothesis seems more plausible. Mexico rushed to hand over El Chapo to Obama to prevent Trump from taking credit for the extradition. As Mexican journalist Esteban Illades argued, if Mexico had delayed the extradition by one more day, Trump would have boasted about his role in organising it for months on Twitter.

But Trump didn't pay attention to Peña Nieto's warning: two days after taking office, he announced that he would begin renegotiating NAFTA with the leaders of Canada and Mexico, and set a meeting with Peña Nieto on January 31.

Peña Nieto sent Videgaray and Ildefonso Guajardo, Mexico's Minister of Economy, to Washington for preparing his meeting with Trump. He instructed them to avoid both submission and confrontation in negotiations with the American administration.

But that plan faltered when, on the night before the emissaries were to arrive to Washington, Trump tweeted that Wednesday would be a "big day" for "national security" because he was looking forward to "building the wall." Videgaray and Guajardo were actually in the White House when Trump left the building to sign his executive order.

This insult raised outrage in Mexico. Intellectuals, politicians and citizens, both left and right, demanded that Peña Nieto cancel his visit to Washington.

Mexico's president answered this new provocation with a short video statement, in which he said that Mexican consulates would now serve as legal aid offices for undocumented Mexican migrants in the US. He resisted though cancelling the meeting with Trump, saying that he would make a decision based on Videgaray's and Guajardo's report out.

But another social media blast from Trump derailed that wait-and-see strategy, too:

Donald J. Trump
@realDonaldTrump
of jobs and companies lost. If Mexico is unwilling to pay for the badly needed wall, then it would be better to cancel the upcoming meeting.

Even for mild Peña Nieto this was too much. He cancelled the meeting with Trump without even a press conference. Instead he tweeted: "This morning we have informed the White House that I will not attend the working meeting with @POTUS scheduled next Tuesday."

As Foreign Minister Videgaray acknowledged, "You don't ask your neighbour to pay for your home's wall."

A phone call between Trump and Peña Nieto on Friday morning may allow for a brief cooling-off period, but without a doubt Mexico and the US have entered into an age of conflict. The consequences, in North America and beyond, are still uncertain.

Spectres of the National Anthem

If the US administration moves forward with its proposed plan to build the wall and fund it by imposing a 20% tax on Mexican imports, Peña Nieto's government has options for retaliation. It could implement a crackdown on American citizens—many of them retirees—who overstay their tourist visas in Mexico, or impose reciprocal tariffs on American exports.

Indeed, the US should not take Mexican friendship for granted. As Mexican historian Enrique Krauze has pointed out, despite recent good relations, Mexico has a series of historical grievances against the US, which remain deeply rooted in Mexican collective memories.

First, the US invaded Mexico in 1846, annexing half of its territory. This event was so traumatic that it became the main theme of the Mexican national anthem.

Then, in 1913, the American ambassador Henry Lane Wilson plotted to have democratically elected president Francisco Madero murdered. This incident plunged Mexico into a fierce civil war and postponed effective implementation of democracy in the country for 90 years.

Finally, in 1914 US marines occupied the city of Veracruz, triggering a prolonged period of hostile relations. The bond between Mexico and the US only normalised again in 1942 with Franklin D. Roosevelt's Good Neighbour policy.

To maintain this peaceful coexistence, both Mexican and American governments have usually taken into account the complex historic relationship between the countries.

Trump's novelty is that he seemingly has no interest in or intention to contemplate the conflicted history of Mexican-American relations—not even considering the strategic importance of Mexico for his nation.

The Twitter President

Instead, his policy decisions seem based on social media metrics. Mexican writer Jorge Volpi believes that Trump's use of Twitter as a privileged medium says a lot about this president. Twitter favours speed over analysis, wit over depth, and aggression over reflection. For Volpi, these are very Trumpian character traits.

The global consequences of such Twitter diplomacy are unknowable. But in Mexico, beyond generating a diplomatic crisis, Trump's actions are successfully arousing the dormant spirits of Mexican nationalism.

Social media platforms are on fire there. Denise Dresser, a respected liberal intellectual, declared that though Donald Trump's presidency may last eight years, Mexico has existed for thousands of years. The historian Rafael Estrada Michel has called for Mexico to renegotiate not NAFTA but the Guadalupe-Hidalgo treaty, which established the current US-Mexico border after the Mexican-American war.

If US-Mexico relations continue in this line, Mexicans will be forced to pay a terrible price for Trump's antics. NAFTA established a prosperous free-trade zone in North America, and without its main trade partner, Mexico will have to entirely reinvent its global alliances and its economic structure.

By the way, according to the Office of the US Trade Representative website—which, in our brave new world of alternative facts, might be taken down soon—US manufacturing exports have increased 258% under NAFTA, and 40% of Mexican exports into the US are actually originated in American inputs.

It is also likely that the US will find it seeking Mexico's support in the near future. Neighbourly collaboration is still necessary to face the myriad challenges both countries share, including climate change and cross-border drug policy. Will Mexico be there next time the US needs it?

It now falls on American and Mexican citizens to defend and foster the peaceful relationship that has been built with much suffering over decades—not with Twitter diplomacy, but with human feeling.

Social Media Can Be Too Informal to Be Effective

Michelle Bovée

Michelle Bovée is the market intelligence manager at MAGNA Global.

Over two years ago, I wrote a critique of the then newly-elected Prime Minister of India Narendra Modi's use of Twitter to respond publicly to the world leaders who had reached out to congratulate him on his success. Modi's tweets were strategic, with close allies, such as Canada and Japan, receiving early mentions, while those with whom the Prime Minister had frostier relations, such as the United States, forced to wait. I concluded that tweets would never replace traditional diplomatic channels, though it could be used for soft power—that is, boosting likeability and demonstrating confidence. However, I did caution that any perceived misstep on Twitter would forever be available for over-analysis and dissection in the 24-hour news cycle.

Clearly, I did not predict Donald Trump. In the weeks following the election, he has become known for using Twitter as a channel for foreign policy declarations, having used the social media service to share his opinions on nuclear weapons, the functionality of the UN, Israel, and China's supposed drone-stealing practices, among a myriad of other topics of international significance. His frequent commenting on sensitive international relations topics in 140 characters or less has already drawn China's ire, prompting Xinhua, the state-run news organization, to publish an article titled: "Addiction to Twitter diplomacy is unwise." This article was released following a tweet suggesting that China has been draining US resources but refuses to help with North Korea—though he does not specify *how* China might assist with North Korean relations, or how China is taking money from the United States. Getting

"Twitter Diplomacy: Hardly a Bold New World for Foreign Policy," by Michelle Bovée, Charged Affairs, January 23, 2017. Reprinted by permission.

such granularity from a tweet is impossible, given the character limits: one of the many pitfalls of relying on Twitter diplomacy.

Some, like Newt Gingrich, have praised Trump's unorthodox approach to foreign policy. Gingrich called the use of Twitter "brilliant," and suggested we get used to Trump making key policy announcements via social media, simply because "this is who he [Trump] is," and he is not going to change. Though now that Trump has been sworn into office, he may find that he does have to change in order to be taken seriously as a world leader. It is one thing to rile up China through a series of angry tweets, but it's another thing entirely to use those tweets as the basis of a coherent foreign policy doctrine that includes follow through and sparks change. If anything, it seems possible that China would be the one to follow through with a forceful response, since the Communist Party has been taking steps for years to understand public opinion and leverage that information to inform policy.

However, China is not the only one who would be concerned with a foreign policy based around social media declarations. Chatter about sensitive topics like nuclear policy, now that Trump is in office, would send a signal to other leaders that few issues are off the table when it comes to tweeting, which could, in turn, discourage them from meeting with the new president, for fear their conversations would become public. The same can be said of a foreign policy doctrine that includes reliance on any type of social media site, including Facebook or personal blogs, to discuss issues that affect national and international policy.

Gingrich is right about one thing: by using Twitter, Trump is able to, "very quickly, over and over again … set the agenda." His unprompted remarks on various foreign policy topics have consistently made the 24-hour news cycle, sent policy wonks scrambling to find meaning and make predictions, and prompted foreign leaders to issue official responses. Twitter diplomacy creates a global conversation in a way that typical diplomatic channels and White House press briefings do not. The tweets come straight from the source, and everyone has a chance to respond directly (though whether or not Trump sees those responses is another question) and share their thoughts with the rest of the global Twitter community.

This platform seems more suited to Modi's form of Twitter diplomacy, since he did not rely on the platform to discuss complex, nuanced topics that require well-thought out statements and in-depth negotiations like Israeli-Palestinian relations and nuclear proliferation. Modi's tweets include comments such as, "India will remain a beacon of peace & progress, stability & success, and access & accommodation" and "I pray that those injured in the accident in Etah recover at the earliest." Trump's Twitter history, on the other hand, contains remarks such as "the concept of global warming was created by and for the Chinese in order to make US manufacturing non-competitive," which is deliberately provoking a foreign power without any form of evidence.

Trump has promised to be "very restrained" on Twitter, and now that he has officially been sworn in, I, for one, hope that is the case. As a private citizen, Trump's use of Twitter to rant about foreign nations was comical, but, as a world leader, that same use could have serious ramifications, from provoking other countries into altering their policies towards the United States to discouraging them from entering into discussions with the President. Perhaps the best we can all do is unfollow him.

Social Media Can Be Part of Diplomacy, but Direct Engagement Is Still Necessary

Constance Duncombe

Constance Duncombe is a researcher and lecturer at Monash University in Australia.

The attention given to each "unpresidential" tweet by US President Donald Trump illustrates the political power of Twitter. Policymakers and analysts continue to raise numerous concerns about the potential political fall-out of Trump's prolific tweeting. Six months after the inauguration, such apprehensions have become amplified.

Take for instance Trump's tweet in March 2017 that "North Korea is behaving very badly. They have been 'playing' the United States for years. China has done little to help!," posted on the eve of US Secretary of State Rex Tillerson's first official visit to China. The tweet complicated an already fractious relationship that Tillerson claimed was at "an inflection point." Another example is Trump's tweet on 24 January, 2017, regarding US national security and building the proposed US-Mexico border wall—"big day planned on NATIONAL SECURITY tomorrow. Among other things, we will build the wall!" This tweet signalled a steep decline in US-Mexico relations leading to Mexican President Enrique Peño Nieta's cancellation of a planned meeting with Trump scheduled for the next week.

Such apprehension about the political effects of Twitter have often been linked to characterizations of the micro-blogging service itself as promoting overly negative, irrational, and unmoderated communication. There have even been calls to stop reading so much into Trump's tweets. Yet we cannot deny that social media

"How Twitter Enhances Conventional Practices of Diplomacy," by Constance Duncombe, Oxford University Press, October 5, 2017, https://blog.oup.com/2017/10/twitter-diplomacy-practices-foreign-policy/. By permission of Oxford University Press.

is increasingly used in diplomacy, and Twitter is especially rising in popularity as a foreign policy tool.

The power of Twitter emerges through how it challenges conventional diplomatic practices. Political leaders and policymakers frequently use Twitter alongside formal assemblies, social gatherings, and unofficial meetings, which have exemplified diplomacy over time. Two important aspects of Twitter stand out in facilitating this change: firstly, the public nature of tweets means an initial exchange between Twitter users can be shared with a much larger audience, leading to an incredible level of scrutiny. Secondly, the speed of this communication means there is much less time to digest and evaluate information, which can lead to a slow realization of change.

One noticeable outcome of the rapid and public nature of Twitter as a diplomatic tool is the insights it can provide into patterns of representations of both state identity and emotional expression, which are in turn central to the signalling of intentions between adversaries. How a state represents itself and recognizes others, often through boundaries of "us and them," can be imbued with emotions that signal particular foreign policy positions.

Consider a well-publicized acrimonious Twitter exchange between Greek Prime Minister Alexis Tsipras and Turkish Prime Minister Davutoğlu in November 2015, during the EU-Turkey refugee summit. Tsipras publically "trolled" Davutoğlu over Turkey's continued violation of Greek airspace and its apparent reluctance to find a solution to the refugee crisis in the Aegean Sea: "To Prime Minister Davutoğlu: Fortunately our pilots are not as mercurial as yours against the Russians #EUTurkey." Davutoğlu tweeted back that "comments on pilots by @tsipras seem hardly in tune with the spirit of the day. Alexis: let us focus on our positive agenda." Using representations of Turkey as unpredictable and volatile, Tsipras signaled continued Greek frustrations with Turkish actions. Davutoğlu, on the other hand, avoided escalating tensions further between the two states by framing his response within a positive affective disposition, calling for greater cooperation and understanding.

Another case of Twitter's role in transformational diplomacy that stands out is Iran and US engagement via the microblogging platform in the lead up to the historic Iran and P5+1 nuclear deal in 2015, which saw sanctions against Iran lifted in exchange for a drawing down of its nuclear program.

Twitter played 2 key roles during this deal.

Firstly, Twitter became an alternative platform to official communication through which key stakeholders—US Secretary of State John Kerry, Iranian Foreign Minister Javad Zarif, Iranian President Hassan Rouhani, and Ayatollah Khamenei—could communicate and "talk honestly" with one another, arguably helping to develop stronger trust between these counterparts. Consider the Iranian response to the open letter signed by 47 US Senate Republicans in April 2015, which claimed any executive agreement on the nuclear issue made between Obama and Khamenei could be swiftly revoked. Zarif tweeted directly to the instigator of the letter, US Senator Tom Cotton: "ICYMI my response. In English." This tweet included a full page rejoinder emphasizing Iran's good faith involvement in the nuclear negotiations. Zarif's use of Twitter to reach out publically to Cotton allowed for a clear challenge to the representation of Iran as threatening and irrational. In doing so, Iran was able to openly advocate for continued diplomatic efforts from all parties to the nuclear negotiations, signaling Iranian resolve to reach an acceptable deal.

Secondly, Twitter provided an alternative platform through which Iran could introduce slight shifts in representations of itself and the US. Key tropes of mutual respect proved to be a win-win; Iran as peaceful and progressive, and the negotiations were an instrumental opportunity in shifting the focus of Iranian communications to promoting positive aspects of its identity, rather than continually emphasizing negative representations of the US. This was a significant and public shift in the dynamics of recognition between these two states. These representations are key to understanding how, despite deep historical animosities on both sides, a more positive relationship was built that resulted in a successful nuclear deal. Unfortunately, Trump's tweets about the "terrible" nuclear deal demonstrate how easily, and quickly, good attempts at conflict resolution can be undermined. Representations that are deeply ingrained can also be easily deployed on social media, leading to greater potential for hostility.

Ultimately, diplomacy will continue to unfold through time-honored practices of engagement between states. However, dismissing the role of social media as a diplomatic engagement tool, particularly Twitter, means potential openings for transformative change might well pass before they can be acted upon.

CHAPTER 4

Can Diplomacy and Hard Power Be Used Together?

The Use of Power Requires Many Tools

Aigerim Raimzhanova

Aigerim Raimzhanova received her doctorate from the University of Bucharest's Institute for Cultural Diplomacy.

[…]

In view of all the issues with soft power, one should not be hasty in abandoning other types of power. Evidently, soft power can be derived from a broad range of sources, but successfully leveraging it can only be achieved through a careful and balanced approach. The governments need to understand their soft power assets, see whether they can be mobilized by the state, and, if so, where and how they might be deployed (McClory, 2011: 5). The new global paradigm makes renegotiation of international relations and reshaping of policies are very important (Bound et al, 2007). However, ultimately, one needs to realize that soft power cannot be a remedy recipe for all the cases. Some foreign policy objectives are better suited to soft power strategies, while others are not and, therefore, the specialists must establish clear objectives. An important consideration is to ask what the initiatives and power is used for (Nye, 1990: 160). Any power decision requires a careful assessment of different factors. Pallaver (2011: 97–99) rationalizes the decision-making process and the choice of power frames in four-steps: understanding the context, appropriate power choice, the effectiveness of power solution for the outcomes, and the successful implementation of agenda.

Wergin (2014) of the *New York Times* argues that, in case of the US, for instance, soft power cannot replace hard power. According to him, soft power is merely a complementary foreign policy tool that can yield results only when it is backed up by real might. This brings up a question, whether you need soft power at all, if you have

"Power in IR: Hard, Soft, and Smart," by Aigerim Raimzhanova, ICD - Institute for Cultural Diplomacy, December 2015. Reprinted by permission.

a strong hard power. The intuition—in current global climate—
would be yes, since becoming influential in the international
relations of the 21st century will require shaping narratives, setting
international norms and mobilizing transnational networks. The
credibility and the maintenance of international support is the
essence of soft power (Nye, 2004: 8–9).

The current reality of the international relations demonstrates
that it is necessary to approach soft and hard power together, rather
than separately. In fact, the classic distinction between realpolitik
and liberalism becomes blurred; hard power and soft power often
interact and reinforce each other (Nye, 1990; Nye, 2004). Both are
ultimately related because they both represent the ability to achieve
a desired goal by affecting the behavior of others and, thus, are
inextricably intertwined (Nye, 2004).

The ability to skilfully combine hard and soft power for the
development of integrated strategies is called smart power (Nye
and Armitage, 2007: 7). In other words, smart power is the capacity
of an actor to combine elements of hard power and soft power in
ways that the actor's goals are advanced effectively and efficiently
(Wilson, 2008: 115). Soft power alone may not be sufficient, but
its relative strategic importance compared to hard power will
continue to increase (McClory, 2011: 24). Smart power advocates
need to articulate the advantages of hard power, such as strong
military, in combination with investing in alliances, partnerships
and institutions. If hard power is "push" and soft power is "pull,"
the combination allows leveraging maximum results in a legitimate
way (Nye, 2011b: 19). As an approach that goes further hard and
soft, it fits well into the current realm of international relations.

Smart power can take on different forms. What has been called
smart power is in fact a combination of diplomatic, economic,
military, political, legal and cultural tools, and the European Union
could be regarded as one of the best examples of this (Pallaver,
2011: 20). Manners (2000) defines EU's power as normative power
because of its ability to shape international norms in its own image.
The EU, like many political actors, has the economic tools and

military power, but the author suggests that these are secondary to its ability to shape what passes for normal in international relations, and which undoubtedly has utilitarian, social, moral, and narrative dimensions to it (Manners, 2000: 31).

Given the complexity of the conceptual, institutional, political, and cultural issues, smart power will not be easy to achieve in the short term (Wilson, 2008: 122). First and foremost, however, smart power is the recognition of the different forms of power and the instruments it can employ. As a newly discovered concept, smart power requires further studies. However, one can logically propose that, if hard and soft power has its resources, so does smart power. This paper will look at smart through its resources, not as an ability or combine hard and soft power resources. The author accepts that smart power is an ability to combine two forms of power; however, also views smart power through its resources. Hence, in the context of this paper, smart power resource is defined as a tool that can attribute to both hard and soft power.

[...]

Hard and Soft Power Both Have a Role to Play

William Inboden is an academic who serves as executive director and William Powers Jr. Chair of the Clements Center for National Security at the University of Texas at Austin.

One of the few core responsibilities of the federal government mandated by the Constitution of the United States is "to provide for the common defence." Upon commissioning, every American military officer swears an oath to "support and defend" this Constitution. Accordingly, the core mission of the American military is to protect and defend our nation. This means deterring potential aggressors and, if deterrence fails, fighting and winning wars. Any consideration of the military's role and American defense policy must start with that foundational principle.

Yet if the need for a strong military begins with the mission to fight and win wars, it does not end there. As the quote from Theodore Roosevelt at the beginning of this essay illustrates, American leaders have long appreciated that a formidable military can produce abundant diplomatic and economic dividends, even—especially—when not wielded in wartime. The United States' military capability supported our nation's rise to global greatness over the past century, but this was often because of the increased influence and credibility produced by this capability rather than the overt use of force. Along the way, there developed an American strategic tradition that integrated military strength with diplomatic acumen, economic growth, and international influence. It is an historic tradition with an impressive heritage and continuing salience today.

Drawing on the historical record, there are many ways beyond the kinetic use of force that a strong national defense bolsters our

"The Role of a Strong National Defense," by William Inboden, The Heritage Foundation, 2015. Reprinted by permission.

national power and global influence. A robust defense budget and defense policy also strengthens our nation in manifest other ways. A well-equipped defense enhances our capabilities and influence across virtually all other elements of national power: our economy, our diplomacy, our alliances, and our credibility and influence in the world. Conversely, an underresourced national defense threatens to diminish our national power across all of these other dimensions.

A strong national defense is thus indispensable for a peaceful, successful, and free America—even if a shot is never fired. The diplomatic successes in building and maintaining a stable and peaceful international order achieved by the United States over the past century have been enabled by America's military dominance. Conversely, the calamitous defense budget cuts and corresponding rise of potential peer competitors in the present day are already undermining America's diplomatic and economic influence.

A well-appointed military improves diplomacy with adversaries, strengthens our alliances, signals credibility and resolve, deters aggression, and enhances national morale. Yet this is not to disregard the manifest other dividends that a strong military can pay. There are multiple pathways by which investments in military hard power produce economic benefits. For example, the military's role in protecting a stable international environment also creates predictable and secure conditions in which economic growth can flourish. The American security umbrella facilitated Western Europe's postwar reconstruction and economic revival, and Asia's half-century economic boom has been partly a function of America's treaty alliances in the region maintaining peace and stability, exemplified by the United States Navy's Seventh Fleet protecting an open maritime order, freedom of navigation, and secure sea lanes.

Additionally, while America's world-leading economy has largely been generated by free enterprise and private sector–led growth, innovations in defense technology can sometimes have economically beneficial civilian applications. There are numerous examples from the past 75 years of technological innovations that originated as defense projects but were eventually adapted for private-sector commercial use, including nuclear energy, jet propulsion, the Internet, global positioning systems, and unmanned aerial vehicles.

[...]

Insights from History: Signaling Resolve and Supporting Allies (Harry S. Truman)

At first glance, Presidents Theodore Roosevelt and Harry Truman have little in common. One was a Republican, the other a Democrat. One was an East Coast Harvard-educated blue blood from one of America's most distinguished familial lineages, the other a Midwestern small-town haberdasher with only a high school education—the last American President without a college diploma. One was the architect of America's debut at the high table of international politics, the other the befuddled inheritor of America's new role as a global superpower and the architect of many institutions of the new international order.

Yet Roosevelt and Truman also shared much in common, including a belief in American exceptionalism, a commitment to the universality of liberty and preserving and extending free societies, and especially an appreciation for the role a strong military plays in projecting power and influence, even without the use of lethal force. As with Roosevelt, most of Truman's enduring national security accomplishments came through the adept employment of military power as a diplomatic and economic instrument of statecraft. Just as our nation still benefits from the international institutions and postwar order he helped to create, there is also much to learn from his integration of a strong defense into the larger structure of national power.

Upon taking the oath of office in April 1945, Truman was bequeathed a situation unprecedented in its complexity and challenges. In short order, he had to navigate:

- The decision to drop the atomic bomb on Japan;
- The end of World War II and the unconditional surrender settlements that would give the United States near-total control of the reconstruction of Germany and Japan;
- The crafting of a postwar international political and economic order that would preserve stability and promote prosperity and ordered liberty; and
- The emerging Cold War with the Soviet Union and its sundry satellite states that would loom over the next four decades of American national security policy as the United States sought to contain Soviet expansionism while preventing the belligerent exchange of nuclear warheads.

It was a tall order for even the most seasoned statesman, let alone a relatively untested and ill-equipped Senator from Missouri.

To appreciate Truman's strategic innovations, one should recall the fraught and unprecedented international climate of the time. The United States and Soviet Union had fought together as allies in World War II, yet even as the war wound down in 1945, tensions between the two victors emerged over the contours of the postwar order. By the next year, it was becoming clear that Soviet dictator Josef Stalin regarded the United States as an adversary and had aggressive designs to dominate Eastern Europe and points beyond.

This left American leaders struggling to formulate a response amidst what appeared to be the unpalatable choices of either fighting the Soviet Union or acquiescing to the further expansion of Communist tyranny. Yale historian John Lewis Gaddis aptly described it as "the despair of 1946 when war or appeasement appeared to be the only alternatives open to the United States." Furthermore, with the end of the war, many feared the prospect of slipping back into the economic depression that had plagued the 1930s.

Into this environment of anxiety and policy uncertainty, George Kennan sent his renowned "Long Telegram" from Moscow, diagnosing Soviet intentions and advocating what became the strategy of containment. Instead of fight or flight, containment offered the option of resisting Soviet aggression without triggering a third world war. But while Kennan may have developed containment as a concept, it took Truman's leadership and vision to operationalize and implement it in practice.

The success of containment depended largely, though by no means exclusively, on the non-kinetic use of military power. Kennan himself appreciated this. In a 1946 address at the National War College, the lifelong diplomat told his audience, "You have no idea how much it contributes to the politeness and pleasantness of diplomacy when you have a little quiet armed force in the background." As Gaddis points out:

> [T]he mere existence of such forces, [Kennan] wrote two years later, "is probably the most important single instrumentality in the conduct of US foreign policy." A Policy Planning Staff study done under Kennan's direction in the summer of 1948 concluded that armed strength was essential as a means of making political positions credible, as a deterrent to attack, as a source of encouragement to allies, and, as a last resort, as a means of waging war successfully should war come.

Truman's Cold War policy incorporated these insights. From the Marshall Plan, to the creation of NATO, to the passage of the National Security Act creating the Central Intelligence Agency and National Security Council, to the issuance of seminal strategy blueprints such as NSC-68, the Truman Administration created a national and international set of institutions that leveraged military power into diplomatic and economic influence. Two Truman initiatives especially illustrate this concept: the Truman Doctrine providing aid to Greece and Turkey and the Berlin Airlift.

Truman's 1947 address to Congress is best remembered for his declaration that "it must be the policy of the United States to support free peoples who are resisting attempted subjugation by armed minorities or by outside pressures." Less appreciated is how the actual aid packages he developed for Greece and Turkey leveraged American military power to strengthen beleaguered allies and signal American resolve to Stalin. Unlike the Marshall

Plan announced later that year, which provided economic reconstruction aid to Western Europe, the Greece and Turkey assistance packages also included a substantial military component to help the governments of the two Mediterranean nations defeat Communist insurgencies.

This had not been a foregone conclusion. Several of Truman's advisers argued for limiting the packages to economic aid, but Truman sided with then-Under Secretary of State Dean Acheson's arguments for including military hardware and advisers. This reflected Truman's belief in what political scientist Henry Nau calls "armed diplomacy" and had far-reaching implications. For example, the aid to Turkey included establishment of the Joint American Military Mission to Aid Turkey (JAMMAT), an ambitious Defense Department initiative that transformed the Turkish military and established a template for eventual American military assistance programs with other allies.

The robust American military aid to Greece and Turkey would not have been possible without the expertise and military technology that the United States developed during World War II. In finishing the war as the most dominant military power on the planet, even in the midst of rapid demobilization, the US still had considerable defense resources to employ in support of its friends, allies, and interests. Truman fused military hardware, economic aid, and vigorous diplomacy into a new tool to implement his Cold War strategy. In doing so, he also ushered in a new era in American power projection. The incorporation of military assistance into the program of aid to Greece and Turkey sent a strong signal of American resolve to the Soviet Union and its satellites while also shoring up important American allies during their periods of acute vulnerability.

The next year, an even more vexing challenge emerged when the Soviet Union made an audacious power grab and cut off Western access to West Berlin, the portion of the German capital isolated within the Communist-controlled occupation zone that would eventually become East Germany. Eschewing either a diplomatic capitulation or a violent escalation, Truman instead ordered a massive airlift to provide food, medicine, and other living essentials to the beleaguered citizens of West Berlin. American military cargo planes operated these resupply flights around the clock for the next 11 months until an embarrassed Stalin backed down and lifted the blockade.

Again, this non-kinetic use of military power had the intended effect of signaling American resolve to Stalin while simultaneously reassuring and strengthening the allied city of West Berlin. This was no mere humanitarian gesture. As Henry Nau has observed, Truman's "decision to erect Berlin as the outpost of Western freedom was monumental. It … placed American forces at risk to defend the 'disputed' borders of freedom in Europe" and "was a preeminent example of the preemptive use of force to deter aggression."

While one might not normally consider cargo planes delivering food aid to civilians to be the "preemptive use of force," Nau has it exactly right. Truman deployed American military resources in a formidable display of resolve, at considerable risk, to dissuade the Soviets from their attempted seizure of West Berlin. It was a turning point in the Cold War, as it revealed the Soviet Union's malign intentions as well as the limits of Soviet adventurism. It galvanized American allies and led directly to the demands of several Western European nations to create what soon became the North Atlantic Treaty Organization (NATO). Without a shot being fired, the American military achieved a significant diplomatic success and made a formidable display of American power.

[…]

Diplomacy Is Strengthened by Military Power

Senator Rand Paul and Isaac Applbaum

Rand Paul is a US senator from Kentucky. Isaac Applbaum is a global technology investor and pro-Israel activist.

Peace through strength. It's a philosophy that guided the United States to victory in the Cold War and a policy that protected us from the calamity of nuclear war. But in the heated debate over Syria, our commitment to this approach has wavered—and it's time we reasserted its prominence.

Some say that America's credibility was threatened when President Barack Obama drew a red line on the use of chemical weapons and then allowed the Syrians to cross it without repercussions. We couldn't disagree more—that would be a profound misreading of Obama's response to the Syrian civil war. Our nation's democratic principles give priority to the voice of individual liberties and freedoms. We will defend them with all of our nation's might. We will not allow any nation or group to terrorize the free world—now or ever.

But foreign policy can often be a jumble of contradictions. Global enemies of the last decade can be our allies in today's conflicts. Our friends could be our enemies tomorrow. As a result, we need to evaluate each foreign policy situation on its own merits and be open to new ideas—new approaches to resolve old conflicts.

The world is changing quickly. Americans are now targets in Kenya. The great civilizations of the last millennium are descending into chaos. Christians are being attacked in Syria and Pakistan. Jews are being attacked in European cities, and Israelis now don gas masks in preparation of the regionalization of the Syrian conflict.

"Peace Through Strength," by Sen. Rand Paul and Isaac Applbaum, *Foreign Policy*, October 15, 2013. Reprinted by permission.

As the same time, we've also seen rapid diplomatic developments in the war in Syria that show the power of blending our military might with aggressive diplomacy. We should seek to repeat this elsewhere—and it should start with Iran.

As Western nations sit down with Iran this week in Geneva, we should vigorously support efforts to negotiate a diplomatic solution that ensures Iran has no nuclear weapon capability and that it does not share its technology with other nations. We should also maintain—and even strengthen—the sanctions that have helped to bring Iran back to the negotiation table. And yes, we should keep all options on the table to ensure that Iran is not just stalling for time, but truly being transparent about its technology and its intentions.

The world should be on notice: the United States will act with overwhelming force if it is attacked—or if vital national security interests are at stake.

In the case of the Syrian civil war, there is no clear American interest. In fact, US intervention might upset the stability of the region and work against our national security interests. By going into a war on the same side as al Qaeda and other Islamic extremists, we might end up aiding the cause that attacked America on 9/11. While Syrian President Bashar al-Assad is clearly a bad guy, there is no clear military objective in Syria.

Still, some argue that North Korea and Iran could be emboldened if the United States elects not to use force against Assad.

This is simply not true. North Korea sits atop a stockpile of weapons in close proximity to tens of thousands of US troops. If Pyongyang ever used these weapons against our troops, they would see a massive response from the United States. The American people would be united, and Congress would declare war in a heartbeat. For anyone to think otherwise—be they a hawkish American pundit or a North Korean despot—is crazy.

Likewise, Iran—or any nation developing nuclear weaponry—should not doubt the military strength and unified approach of the American people toward the terrorizing of US citizens and allies in Asia, Africa, Europe, and the Middle East. Nor should these nations doubt that international resolve will coalesce and extract harsh penalties on nations that pursue these activities. Ultimately, the United States cannot and will not take any option off the table in order to protect Israel and other regional democracies, and to deter Tehran from acquiring a nuclear weapon.

Going forward, the United States should dramatically increase our political and diplomatic efforts to halt Iran's nuclear weapons program, and we should do so alongside all interested parties. Russia and China both trade with Iran and will be a key part of the solution.

Iran will be the next test for US foreign policy after Syria. The administration should re-engage now—it can't simply sit back and wait until a military strike is the only option. This will mean employing carrots as well as sticks—like harsher sanctions but openness to dialogue. This will mean transparent inspections of nuclear facilities that yield trustworthy information or additional consequences that guarantee Iran isn't just playing for time. We need to ensure the Iranian regime gets clear messages about the ramifications of any hostility towards America, Israel, or regional allies.

Peace through strength is not a lonely position. In fact, there are numerous voices in the United States and in Israel calling for more political and diplomatic pressure and engagement. And many are cautioning against an Iranian (or Syrian) policy that focuses exclusively on a preemptive strike—including a former US Army Chief of Staff, a former head of the US Air Force, and recent heads of the Mossad and Shin Bet.

American foreign policy leaders should heed this advice—and learn the lessons of recent entanglements. We can and must use military force when necessary, and be willing to leave the option on the table when our security is threatened. However, we also need to engage politically and diplomatically to further our interests—as well as the interests of our allies—as long and as often as possible.

In the past, America's winning strategy was to seek peace through strength. It's a philosophy that served us back then—and one that will serve us again in the future.

Hard Power Alone Is Not Enough

Joseph Nye

Joseph Nye is an American political scientist and cofounder of the theory of neoliberalism, which was developed in 1977 in his book Power and Interdependence, *coauthored by Robert Keohane. He is a member of the Defense Policy Board.*

Traditionally, the test of a great power was "strength for war." War was the ultimate game in which the cards of international politics were played and estimates of relative power were proven. Over the centuries, as technologies evolved, the sources of power have shifted.

Today, the foundations of power have been moving away from the emphasis on military force. A combination of factors— nuclear weapons that are too awesome to use, the difficulties of building empires in an age of nationalism, the unwillingness of western societies to send their troops into battle—have conspired to make war a last resort for most advanced countries. In the words of British diplomat Robert Cooper, "A large number of the most powerful states no longer want to fight or conquer." War remains possible, but it is much less acceptable now than it was even half a century ago.

For most of today's great powers, the use of force would jeopardise their economic objectives. Even non-democratic countries that feel moral constraints on the use of force have to consider its effects on their economic objectives. As Thomas Friedman has put it, countries are disciplined by an "electronic herd" of investors who control their access to capital in a globalised economy.

Force remains important as we saw on September 11, 2001 and in Afghanistan. But it is also important to mobilise international

"Why Military Power Is No Longer Enough," by Joseph Nye, Guardian News and Media Limited, March 30, 2002. Reprinted by permission.

coalitions and build institutions to address shared threats and challenges. As I explain in my book *The Paradox of American Power: Why the world's Superpower can't go it Alone*, no country today is great enough to solve the problem of global terrorism alone.

There is also an indirect way to exercise power. A country may secure the outcomes it wants in world politics because other countries aspire to its level of prosperity and openness. It is just as important to set the agenda in world politics and attract others as it is to force them to change through the threat or use of military or economic weapons. This aspect of power is "soft power"—getting people to want what you want.

Wise parents know that if they have brought up their children with the right values, their power will be greater than if they have relied only on cutting off allowances or taking away the car keys. Similarly, political leaders and thinkers such as Antonio Gramsci have long understood the power that comes from determining the framework of a debate. If I can get you to want to do what I want, then I do not have to force you to do what you do not want to do.

Soft power is not simply the reflection of hard power. The Vatican did not lose its soft power when it lost the Papal States in Italy in the nineteenth century. Conversely, the Soviet Union lost much of its soft power after it invaded Hungary and Czechoslovakia, even though its economic and military resources continued to grow. Imperious policies that utilised Soviet hard power actually undercut its soft power. And countries like the Canada, the Netherlands, and the Scandinavian states have political clout that is greater than their military and economic weight because of their support for international aid and peace-keeping.

The countries that are likely to gain soft power are those closest to global norms of liberalism, pluralism, and autonomy; those with the most access to multiple channels of communication; and those whose credibility is enhanced by their domestic and international performance. These dimensions of power give a strong advantage to the United States and Europe.

By the late 1930s, the Roosevelt administration became convinced that "America's security depended on its ability to speak to and to win the support of people in other countries." With World War II and the Cold War, the government sponsored efforts including the United States Information Agency, the Voice of America and the Fulbright student exchange programme.

But much soft power arises from forces outside government control. Even before the Cold War, "American corporate and advertising executives, as well as the heads of Hollywood studios, were selling not only their products but also America's culture and values, the secrets of its success, to the rest of the world."

There are areas, such as the Middle East, where ambivalence about, or outright opposition to, American culture limits its soft power. All television in the Arab world used to be state-run until tiny Qatar allowed a new station, Al-Jazeera, to broadcast freely, and it proved wildly popular in the Middle East. Its uncensored images, ranging from Osama bin Laden to Tony Blair, have had a powerful political influence. Bin Laden's ability to project a Robin Hood image enhanced his soft power with some Muslims around the globe. As an Arab journalist described the situation earlier, "Al-Jazeera has been for this intifada what CNN was to the Gulf War." In the eyes of Islamic fundamentalists, the openness of Western culture is repulsive. But for much of the world, including many moderates and young people, our culture still attracts. To the extent that official policies at home and abroad are consistent with democracy, human rights, openness, and respect for the opinions of others, the United States and Europe will benefit from the trends of this global information age, although pockets of fundamentalism will persist and react in some countries.

Power in the global information age is becoming less coercive among advanced countries. But most of the world does not consist of post-industrial societies, and that limits the transformation of power. Much of Africa and the Middle East remains locked in pre-industrial agricultural societies with weak institutions and authoritarian rulers. Other countries, such as China, India, and Brazil, are industrial economies analogous to parts of the West in the mid-twentieth century. In such a variegated world, all three sources of power—military, economic, and soft—remain relevant. However, if current economic and social trends continue, leadership in the information revolution and soft power will become more important in the mix.

Diplomacy Is More Effective than Military Force

Phyllis Bennis

Phyllis Bennis is director of the New Internationalism Project at the Institute for Policy Studies.

What an amazing few weeks we have seen. Not to say everything in my favorite part of the world is suddenly doing fine—Syria and Palestine, Gaza in particular, still face disastrous realities of war and occupation—but suddenly the stand-down on the threat of US missiles in Syria has been joined by a deal on Iran that means moves towards war against Iran are off the table at least for six months, the Geneva II talks on Syria may actually start in the next few weeks, and the war in Afghanistan may actually be coming to an end. Could we be seeing the rising role of diplomacy instead of military force as the basis of US foreign policy?

The Iran Deal

Along with the promise of no additional nuclear-related sanctions, Iran will be allowed to access about $4 billion (out of more than $100 billion being held in western banks) over the next six months. It will be allowed to import spare parts and inspection materials for its civilian aircraft fleet, which has faced serious safety compromises because of the inability to import parts from the US. And it will be allowed to access about $400 million in tuition funds for Iranian students at international universities. It's probably still too soon to give an unequivocal "yes" to that question. But the agreement raises a lot of new—and generally good—possibilities. I wrote about the Iran deal in *The Nation*. There are plenty of problems ahead. The deal is limited, only good for six months, and much

"The Rise of Diplomacy, Not Military Force, in U.S. Foreign Policy?" by Phyllis Bennis, Institute for Policy Studies, December 2, 2013. Reprinted by permission.

of the US-led sanctions regime that has crippled so much of Iran's economy, shredding the middle class, remains in place.

The deal could still fall apart. But both sides are now invested in maintaining it, at least for the six month term, so if the US Congress, Israel, and the Saudis (just to name a few) don't scuttle it, this could be the beginning of something very important. So no war with Iran this week, which could have been a likely result if the negotiations collapsed—thanksgiving indeed!

So what does the deal call for? Negotiated largely by Iranian foreign minister Mohamed Javad Zarif and top European Union envoy Catherine Ashton, though overseen by the US, the deal provides Iran with the promise of no new sanctions and a tiny amount of relief from current sanctions, while freezing and rolling back key components of its nuclear power and research program.

The US and its allies (the other four Permanent Members of the UN Security Council, Britain, China, France, and Russia, plus Germany, thus the "Perm 5 + 1") get far more of their demands met. Iran agreed to completely halt all uranium enrichment over 5%, and to freeze its entire existing arsenal of all uranium enriched above 3.5%. It will dilute or turn into fuel bars its entire arsenal of medium-enriched (20%) uranium. Iran is prohibited from installing any new centrifuges in its enrichment facilities, and can produce only enough centrifuges to replace any that are damaged. It agreed it will not commission, fuel, or produce fuel for the Arak heavy water reactor. And of course Iran's oil sales will continue at 60% below capacity because of the existing sanctions.

Crucially, Iran agreed to far more intrusive inspections by the UN's nuclear watchdog agency. Tehran will provide the IAEA with daily access to its enrichment facilities at Fordow and Natanz, to its centrifuge assembly facilities, uranium mines and more. They will also provide the key information required under the Additional Protocol of the Nuclear Non-Proliferation Treaty (NPT). As a signatory to the NPT, Iran already allows significant inspections of its nuclear facilities. Tehran signed the Additional Protocol in 2003, allowing even greater inspections, but withdrew from the

Protocol (although remaining a signatory to the NPT overall) in 2005 as George Bush's "axis of evil" rhetoric and threats escalated.

Nothing about the current agreement can be taken for granted. Republican and Democratic warmongers alike are threatening to undermine it by imposing new sanctions. Saudi Arabia (while appearing now to have accepted reality) and other Gulf states mobilized powerful opposition, fearing anything that might result in recognition of Iran as a legitimate regional power. And Israel— at least at the political leadership level—continues to threaten unilateral military action against Iran. Israeli Prime Minister Netanyahu called the agreement "a historic mistake."

We need to keep the diplomacy-not-war pressure on. It's highly unlikely (though one should never say impossible!) that Israel will actually move towards a military strike. General Benny Gantz, head of the Israel Defense Forces (IDF), continues to assert that Israel could successfully attack Iran's nuclear sites on its own, even if no other country (read: the United States) supported it.

But there's not too much chance of that happening. Some Israeli officials recognize that an Israeli strike would be dangerous because it would further isolate Tel Aviv from the international community which is overwhelmingly in support of the deal with Iran. But that doesn't mean the Israeli military stays in its barracks. With the Iran agreement a done deal, there's an even greater threat now of a new Israeli attack on Gaza. Netanyahu might do it for domestic political reasons, and certainly engaging in military action, even when Israel starts it unprovoked, is a reliable way to shore up congressional backing in the US.

Beginning November 24 Israel launched a three-day military "exercise" using the coastal city of Ashkelon as a stand-in for Gaza. Netanyahu doesn't HAVE to make a serious case of linkage (he really doesn't even have to claim a serious provocation ...) to gain US support—if it happens, the move will be aimed as much at Congress and the White House as it is the Israeli public and Gaza's 1.8 million civilians imprisoned in the impoverished, crowded Strip. For Congress, it would give many in Congress (although not nearly as many as before) another chance to jump up and remind the world that Israel is our best friend, and that we need to defend/ listen to/agree with Israel on all things. For the White House, it's a message that you ignore/disagree with us at your peril—because now YOU, President Obama, will have to figure out how to respond to our move as well.

As usual, it's up to us to keep the pressure on. We need to make sure the agreement with Iran holds, and we need to make sure the US doesn't continue to exclude Iran from participating in Syria peace talks. (That effort is a really stupid move—if you're serious about diplomacy, everyone who's a major player needs to be at the table. And Iran, key backer of the Syrian regime, is certainly a major player in the Syrian war.)

Palestine

The situation in Gaza continues to deteriorate—even beyond the threat of direct military assault. The Israeli siege—in place since 2007—continues, with almost all goods locked out, and almost all Gazans locked in. And it's worse than ever now, because the network of tunnels on the Gaza-Egypt border, which once provided the basics of consumer goods, fuel, medical and educational supplies, even cars and livestock, are now shut down by the Egyptian military government. Egypt under the current military government has actually destroyed most of the tunnels.

On the "diplomatic" front, the US-sponsored "peace talks" continue staggering along. As many of us have said for far too long, 22 years of failed diplomacy about to turn into 23 is hardly something to write home about. I wrote about the need for Palestinian rights, rather than "arrangements"—some things don't change.One effect of the siege is a huge shortage of fuel for electricity—which Israel, under international law, is obligated to provide. But as is so often the case, when there is no consequence for its violations, the violations continue. My colleague and friend, Richard Falk, the current UN Special Rapporteur on human rights in the occupied territory, recently issued a new urgent warning on the effect of the electricity shortage. Among other things, the lack of fuel means the main sewage treatment plant isn't working—so streets of Gaza city are now flooded with raw sewage. Children—already undernourished and weakened by the siege's cut-off of adequate food and medicine—are wading through sewage on their way to school. Epidemics are almost certain.

For now, the immediate danger is that the success of the Iran negotiations could result in a new military attack on Gaza. If it happens, there is a great danger that the US would simply allow it to go forward, regardless of Israel's violations of both international and US domestic law, as a "gift" to assuage Netanyahu's frustration with being the loser. One thing that might change, on the Palestine-Israel front—I'm now in the running to become Richard Falk's successor as the next UN Special Rapporteur on human rights in the occupied territory. The decision gets made in Geneva, in the Human Rights Council. There are several good people applying, I have no idea what my chances are. But my goal is to continue the extraordinary work Richard has done (and on which I've been privileged to collaborate with him) to engage civil society as a key component of UN engagement and international law. Keep tuned.

Afghanistan—End of the US War?

The US-Afghanistan negotiations over keeping US troops in the country after the "end of combat" in 2014 have hit a new snag. The US-backed president of the country, Hamid Karzai is widely viewed as both corrupt and incompetent (he's not known as the "mayor of Kabul" for nothing, since his brief doesn't extend much beyond the borders of the city). He depends on US money, US support, and US troops to stay in power. But in recent years he's also created a persona of independent, even anti-US posturing, to gain broader public support at home.

With elections scheduled for next spring, Karzai is eager to remain a player so he can help elect his chosen candidate. That may be the most significant reason for his recent rejection of an almost-completed deal with Washington, which would allow around

15,000 US troops to remain in the country after the official end of combat in 2014. Karzai has now staked out a position refusing to grant the US forces immunity from prosecution in Afghan courts for any crimes they might commit. And the US is adamant that without immunity, the troops go home.

This isn't a new idea—it's the same issue that scuttled the potential for keeping US troops in Iraq after the official withdrawal of combat troops. And it led to the complete pull-out of all US troops and all Pentagon-paid contractors in 2011 (although a contingent of State Dept–paid contractors does remain in Iraq even today). In Afghanistan, we might actually see the withdrawal of all US troops after more than twelve years of war and occupation. That wouldn't be a bad thing—it's the first step towards allowing Afghans to reclaim their country. As even the *NY Times* editorial board has now admitted, President Obama has not "explained how a residual force can improve the competency of Afghan forces when a much broader and intensive American engagement over the last decade has not."

Hopefully it will not look like post-withdrawal Iraq, where sectarian and other violence is raging, with more than 6,000 civilians killed this year alone—more than were killed this year in Afghanistan itself. There is no guarantee—but the withdrawal of US troops remains the first and necessary step—only the first—in the long and painful process of allowing people to begin the slow effort of rebuilding their war-shattered lives and their wounded societies.

US reliance on drone attacks in Afghanistan remains central to the US agenda there—which has far more to do with maintaining military bases and the ability to strike at will against anyone the US believes to be a threat to *US* interests, than it does with protecting Afghans from insurgents or others. It's a counter-terrorism agenda based on US concerns, not an effort to win the hearts and minds of Afghans by protecting them. And drone strikes—like those carried out by the CIA in Pakistan, the drone wars in Yemen and Somalia and beyond—are a crucial part of conducting wars with no US casualties, with major US deniability, and with no US accountability. I talked about the US drone wars here. Just a few days ago new US drone strikes in Afghanistan killed civilians, including a child, and severely wounded two women. It is certainly true that many Afghans, mainly those in Kabul and other large cities, would prefer that US troops remain, supposedly for training and to support the large but insufficently trained and armed Afghan military. In the countryside, where the majority of Afghans still live, in small villages and tiny hamlets scattered across isolated and rugged terrain, opposition to the US troops is fierce and growing, primarily because of drone attacks that kill civilians and especially because of night raids on Afghan homes, violating the national and cultural norms of the country. Karzai and US negotiators managed to finesse an agreement on night raids (with weasel language about US troops only being involved in "exceptional circumstances"). And the *loya jirga*, or high council of tribal leaders convened to approve the long-term US troop deal accepted it. But then Karzai pulled his support.

There is certainly a danger that drone strikes would continue even if all US forces are withdrawn from Afghanistan. The work of organizations like Global Drones Watch, initiated by Code Pink in the US, and other anti-drone campaigns remain crucial—not because wars depend on any one weapon, but because focusing on one weapon and the devastation it can impose on children and women and families can be a key component of humanizing the cost of war.

As always, we've got a lot of work to do.

Hard Power Can Undermine Diplomacy

Nathan Gardels

Nathan Gardels is the editor in chief of the WorldPost and a senior adviser at the Berggruen Institute in Los Angeles, California.

A long with other members of the Berggruen Institute's 21st Century Council, I met with President Xi Jinping in Beijing last November on the eve of the Third Plenum of the Central Committee of the Chinese Communist Party.

At that meeting, President Xi outlined the three features of "a new kind of great power relationship":

- No confrontational or zero-sum mentality
- Mutual respect for other's path of development and cultural heritage
- Seek common ground on issues of common interests in pursuit of win-win progress

He greatly impressed our geopolitically diverse group of statesmen, global intellectuals and high-tech entrepreneurs by assuring us that China would avoid "the Thucydides trap"—the kind of rivalry between rising and established powers that led Athens and Sparta to war in ancient times. These were surely words of wisdom and maturity that were heartily appreciated by our group.

But are China's deeds matching President Xi's words?

China's soft power for the last 30 years has rested on two foundations:

- An admirable system of governance that can forge consensus and unity of purpose to see through the long-term implementation of policies on behalf of the Chinese people. This system has enabled hundreds of millions to

"Is China's Hard Power Undermining Its Soft Power?" by Nathan Gardels, The Huffington Post, June 16, 2014. Reprinted by permission.

escape from poverty. Sprawling megacities are rising across China and being linked together by the world's most extensive network of high-speed trains. Schools in Shanghai test the best globally. And China has now recognized it must put its considerable governing capacity and competence behind cleaning up corruption and the environment.

To put the Middle Kingdom's soft power in context, while China is building bullet trains to connect 80 percent of its cities, half of all Indians still lack toilets.

As I have written in my book with Nicolas Berggruen, *Intelligent Governance for the 21st Century: A Middle Way Between West and East,* the Western democracies have much to learn from China's "institutional civilization" and governance model rooted in meritocratic competition from ancient times.

- The "peaceful rise" doctrine first articulated by Zheng Bijian.

In recent months, however, China's surprise, unilateral declaration of an Air Defense Zone, the oil rig anchored in contested waters off of Vietnam, the dispute with the Philippines, the island dispute with Japan and cyberspying for commercial secrets have raised doubts that China's words are matching its deeds. Along with these moves, the ever-deepening embrace of Vladimir Putin's Russia as an ally to counter US presence in the region in the wake of the Crimean annexation suggests a zero-sum and confrontational approach, not the opposite.

None of this is to say that China is singularly at fault or that some of its claims are not legitimate and that others, especially Japan, are not culpable in raising tensions. Everyone now also knows that American NSA cyberspying is globally pervasive.

But it is to say that much of the rest of the world perceives a new confrontational tone in Beijing.

China must be careful not to fall into another more modern trap: letting its hard power undermine the soft power capital it has built up over decades. This is what happened to the US—the pre-emptive attack on Iraq, the Guantanamo prison and the sanctioning of torture undermined America's universal claims. In short, America's hard power undermined its soft power. As a result, American might, both hard and soft, was diminished, not strengthened, by its Iraq adventure—and that is still coming back to haunt it.

As an ancient civilization with a 5,000 year continuous history, as President Xi reminded us in our talk, China should be the adult on the global stage. To bolster its soft power might, it should take an initiating, leadership role in fighting climate change— something that is of vital interest to all of humankind. And it coincides with China's own urgent need to control pollution ruining its environment.

When outlining his new concept of "building on a convergence of interests to create a community of interests," Zheng Bijian rightly focuses on joint action on climate change as a key focus.

American democracy, in particular, is too divided and afflicted by gridlock to offer global leadership on this front. Precisely because of its effective system of governance, China can do what other nations can't.

This would show China's win-win face to the world. Absent this kind of initiative, China risks being identified only with greater assertiveness against its neighbors in East Asia. Acting for the interests of others in a way that coincides with its own would remove mounting doubts that China means what it says about a new kind of great power relationship.

There are many opportunities to work with the United States on climate change even if Washington is paralyzed. As President Obama acknowledged in his own carbon reduction plan announced recently, the US is a federal system with very large states that can determine their own environmental policies. China has provinces that are as large as several European countries.

For example, California and China have already initiated cooperation agreements on pollution reduction in its cities and on climate change, including pilot projects on trading carbon permits with California, the world's largest market for such permits.

In November, California Governor Jerry Brown is planning to host a meeting at Sunnylands—where Presidents Obama and Xi met—to bring together governors from China and the US to develop a common agenda on climate change and pollution reduction at the sub-national level.

It would be a great boost to China's soft power and "win-win" approach if it championed such efforts instead of only let others take the lead.

The Paradox of Soft Power Within China

I would like to briefly make one other salient observation about China and soft power.

Long before Harvard's Joe Nye came up with the idea of "soft power," the Italian Communist Party leader of the early 20th century, Antonio Gramsci, made the distinction between two different kinds of dominant power, or as he put it, hegemony.

For Gramsci, hegemony of the state was based on force, or hard power; the state must establish a monopoly over the means of violence in a society in order to impose and maintain order.

But hegemony in civil society must be based on consent. For Gramsci, the allegiance to a worldview by the public at large must be earned and cannot be enforced. The public must buy into a governing narrative voluntarily or that narrative, by definition, lacks legitimacy.

Please note that neither Gramsci nor I are talking about formal mechanisms of consent, such as elections, but a deeper consent of the rulers and the ruled sharing a common worldview.

In practice, this means the governing power maintains consent through delivering the goods, that is, performance—not just economic, but in terms of overall quality of life. How to organize feedback mechanisms to register consent is a broader issue; one size, for example multi-party elections, does not fit all circumstances and is not always the best form of governance.

For Gramsci, it is soft power, or the consent of civil society, that legitimates hard power, not vice versa. And, for Gramsci, the Communist Party was part of civil society, not the state.

In China the state party has merged these two forms of hegemony, opening the way to blurring force and consent in maintaining power.

From this point of view, the current crackdown on the Internet and bloggers can backfire by undermining, not enhancing, the legitimacy of the governing narrative.

In today's connected world, everyone knows what is going on and shares it with others. To try to censor what everyone already knows by using the force of the state is to that extent undermining voluntary consent in civil society, and thus the legitimacy of the ruling narrative.

I understand that the Chinese Community Party leaders fear the fate of the Soviet Communist Party and do not want to repeat what they see as the mistakes of Gorbachev's "glasnost," or transparency policy.

But this seems to me a misreading of history. The problem in the Soviet Union was not glasnost itself. It was the fact that when you took away the big lies and false fronts through glasnost, there was nothing there. The emperor had no clothes.

China could not be more different. In China, the emperor DOES have clothes. The Party has performed over the last 30 years for the people. And if it continues to do so in an effective way, consent to its rule will continue to be earned.

The paradox is that by trying to avoid the fate of the Soviet party through censorship and a crackdown on the Internet, the Party may well be inviting that very fate, undermining its own legitimacy which must, as Gramsci knew, be based ultimately on consent within civil society.

I was in Moscow often during the years leading up to the collapse of the Soviet Union. I know Gorbachev well and knew Aleksandr Yakovlev—the ideology chief who came up with the glasnost policy—even better. It is manifestly clear from my experience that it was the misguided effort to spin reality, not glasnost, that was the death knell for the Soviet party.

In today's world, legitimacy must come from performance. It is a false belief that consent of the governed can be maintained in our hyper-connected societies by censoring what civil society is supposed to know or not know. The information revolution has consigned that role of the state to the dustbin of history along with the old Soviet party.

Organizations to Contact

The editors have compiled the following list of organizations concerned with the issues debated in this book. The descriptions are derived from materials provided by the organizations. All have publications or information available for interested readers. This list was compiled on the date of publication of the present volume; the information provided here may change. Be aware that many organizations take several weeks or longer to respond to inquiries, so allow as much time as possible.

American Foreign Policy Council (AFPC)
509 C Street NE
Washington, DC 20002
phone: (202) 543-1006
email: afpc@afpc.org
website: https://www.afpc.org

The AFPC is a think tank that provides analysis of US foreign policy and interests around the world, primarily to policy makers. Its research is wide ranging but is conducted through the lens of US foreign policy and how it influences or can be influenced by changing situations around the world.

Atlantic Council
1030 Fifteenth Street NW, 12th Floor
Washington, DC 20005
phone: (202) 778-4952
email: info@AtlanticCouncil.org
website: https://www.atlanticcouncil.org

The Atlantic Council is a think tank focusing on international relations. It publishes research and analysis of international affairs and key issues around the world in order to inform policy makers and foster international security.

Brookings Institution
1775 Massachusetts Avenue NW
Washington, DC 20036
phone: (202) 797-6000
email: communications@brookings.edu
website: https://www.brookings.edu

The Brookings Institution is a wide-ranging think tank and research institute that studies both domestic and international affairs. With experts on a range of topics, Brookings works to inform the public and policy makers about issues defining our world.

Carnegie Council for Ethics in International Affairs (CCEIA)
Merrill House
170 East Sixty-Fourth Street
New York, NY 10065-7478
phone: (212) 838-4120
email: info@cceia.org
website: https://www.cceia.org

The CCEIA focuses on the ethical practice of international affairs, including the ways in which diplomacy can undermine or strengthen human rights protections around the world. Its work includes education programs, publications, and forums focusing on raising awareness of the ethical ways in which states can pursue mutual and individual interests.

Chatham House
Royal Institute of International Affairs
Chatham House
10 St. James's Square
London SW1Y 4LE
United Kingdom
phone: +44 (0)20 7957 5700
email: contact@chathamhouse.org
website: https://www.chathamhouse.org

Chatham House, or the Royal Institute of International Affairs, works to inform policy makers, civil society, and others about international relations practices in order to foster peace and international security. The organization is based in London and is a leading think tank for global studies.

Council on Foreign Relations
58 East Sixty-Eighth Street
New York, NY 10065
phone: (212) 434-9400
email: cfrwashington@cfr.org
website: https://www.cfr.org

The Council on Foreign Relations researches and publishes work on major international affairs issues. Its website includes pages dedicated to specific countries, issues, and important figures, which provide key historical context and expert analysis.

International Institute for Strategic Studies (IISS)
2121 K Street NW, Suite 801
Washington, DC 20037
phone: (202) 659-1490
website: https://www.iiss.org

The IISS is a think tank and research institute that focuses on relations between states. It publishes research, blogs, and other work that examines how states interact, particularly in ways that foster peace. It also publishes data related to diplomacy and conflict.

The Middle East Institute (MEI)
1319 Eighteenth Street NW
Washington, DC 20036
phone: (202) 785-1141
email: info@mei.edu
website: https://www.mei.edu

The MEI is a nonprofit organization dedicated to researching and providing analysis of breaking news in the Middle East and surrounding areas. It publishes work on economics, politics, conflict, and other issues.

United Nations (UN)
405 East Forty-Second Street
New York, NY 10017
phone: (212) 963-1234
website: http://www.un.org

The UN conducts projects and research on conditions around the world and publishes information about key issues in international affairs. The organization has a high level of access to countries other groups are not able to observe or enter, and it has a comprehensive backlog of UN resolutions and decisions passed regarding key issues.

United States Institute of Peace (USIP)
2301 Constitution Avenue NW
Washington, DC 20037
phone: (202) 457-1700
website: https://www.usip.org

The USIP is a think tank studying conflict and international relations. Its experts and researchers conduct studies and analysis of countries around the world, including the ways in which states interact. It also publishes explainers and background information on key issues around the world.

Bibliography

Books

Stephen G. Brooks and William C. Wohlforth, *America Abroad: Why the Sole Superpower Should Not Pull Back from the World*. New York, NY: Oxford University Press, 2016.

Eliot A. Cohen, *The Big Stick: The Limits of Soft Power and the Necessity of Military Force*. New York, NY: Basic Books, 2017.

Michael Cox, *The Post Cold War World: Turbulence and Change in World Politics Since the Fall*. New York, NY: Routledge, 2018.

Dan Drezner, *Theories of International Politics and Zombies*. Princeton, NJ: Princeton University Press, 2014.

Ronan Farrow, *War on Peace: The End of Diplomacy and the Decline of American Influence*. New York, NY: W.W. Norton, 2018.

Lawrence Freedman, *The Future of War: A History*. New York, NY: PublicAffairs, 2017.

Joshua S. Goldstein, *Winning the War on War: The Decline of Armed Conflict Worldwide*. New York, NY: Plume, 2012.

Colin S. Gray, *The Future of Strategy*. New York, NY: Polity Press, 2015.

Richard Haas, *A World in Disarray: American Foreign Policy and the Crisis of the Old Order*. New York, NY: Penguin Press, 2017.

Joshua D. Kertzer, *Resolve in International Politics*. Princeton, NJ: Princeton University Press, 2016.

Gail Dexter Lord and Ngaire Blankenberg, *Cities, Museums and Soft Power*. Washington, DC: American Alliance of Museums, 2015.

Richard McGregor, *Asia's Reckoning: China, Japan, and the Fate of U.S. Power in the Pacific Century.* New York, NY: Viking, 2017.

Jeffrey Robertson, *Diplomatic Style and Foreign Policy: A Case Study of South Korea.* New York, NY: Routledge, 2016.

Angela E. Stent, *The Limits of Partnership: US-Russian Relations in the Twenty-First Century.* Princeton, NJ: Princeton University Press, 2015.

Thomas Wright, *All Measures Short of War: The Contest for the Future of American Power.* New Haven, CT: Yale University Press, 2017.

Periodicals and Internet Sources

John Campbell, "Chinese Soft Power in Africa," Council on Foreign Relations, July 20, 2017. https://www.cfr.org/blog /chinese-soft-power-africa.

Economist, "America's Amateur Diplomats," July 5, 2018. https:// www.economist.com/united-states/2018/07/05/americas -amateur-diplomats.

Economist, "Softly Does It," July 18, 2015. https://www .economist.com/britain/2015/07/18/softly-does-it.

Gardiner Harris, "A Shift from 'Soft Power' Diplomacy in Cuts to the State Dept.," *New York Times,* March 16, 2017. https:// www.nytimes.com/2017/03/16/us/politics/trump-budget -cuts-state-department.html.

Javier C. Hernández, "A Hong Kong Newspaper on a Mission to Promote China's Soft Power," *New York Times,* March 13, 2018. https://www.nytimes.com/2018/03/31/world/asia /south-china-morning-post-hong-kong-alibaba.html.

Zachary Laub, "Hard Power's Essential Soft Side," Council on Foreign Relations, March 29, 2017. https://www.cfr.org /interview/hard-powers-essential-soft-side.

Eric X. Li, "The Rise and Fall of Soft Power," *Foreign Policy*, August 20, 2018. https://foreignpolicy.com/2018/08/20/the -rise-and-fall-of-soft-power.

Reid Standish, "'House of Cards' Is Credible. Just Ask the Russians, Chinese and Iranians," *Washington Post*, October 25, 2018. https://www.washingtonpost.com/outlook /house-of-cards-is-credible-just-ask-the-russians-chinese -and-iranians/2018/10/25/81b02346-d644-11e8-aeb7 -ddcad4a0a54e_story.html?utm_term=.8ed42f1b68f8.

Gerasimos Tsourapas, "How Authoritarian Regimes Use Migration to Exert 'Soft Power' in Foreign Policy," *Washington Post*, July 6, 2018. https://www.washingtonpost .com/news/monkey-cage/wp/2018/07/06/how-authoritarian -regimes-use-migration-to-enact-foreign-policy/?utm _term=.4077bd258241.

Index

U

V

W

X

Y

Z